LAW
FOR
LAY MEN

S.K. Gupta, Advocate

This book is dedicated to ....WE, THE PEOPLE

Preface

The idea of this work arose from the fact that the Law which guides, structures, shapes one's life even before one is born is not taught before one specifically takes it up as a subject for Graduation. The Law, in our civilized society is all pervasive. One can only think of the laws that govern the moment from when the author had the idea of Writing to this work coming into your hands. Law even regulates the rights of Child in womb. But what the law is and how it works is something that is kept away from the very population it is made for.

Science teaches phenomenon of Nature, Mathematics the arithmetic and algebra, Grammar the rules of the Language. All these are taught from beginner schools. But the law which presumes its Knowledge on everyone does not find place in School curriculum.

I Hope the following pages will help one in getting acquainted with the law, some of its basic principles and the method by which it works and further develop a curiosity to know more.

Author

Table of Contents

INTRODUCTORY

1. LAW AND STATE

Law presupposes State. State means an Independent Sovereign Political Unit. In this sense, Uttar Pradesh, Madhya Pradesh are states and so is Union of India and United States of America. Without State, there can be no Law. Though there may exist rules of Conduct such as morality to govern day to day interactions, transactions and procedures. But without the existence of Political Unit (State) all these rules will only be directory in Nature, there being no Imperative enforcing the same. Such moral rules are imbibed in upbringing of the child and are followed throughout the life without much deviation but it is because of personal volition, and not out of compulsion. For such a group of people to become State, they must organize themselves into a Unit, comprising of a Sovereign Head and recognize his supremacy over the subjects.

1.1. Elements of State

State consists of following four constituents -

(i) Population

(ii) Land

(iii) Government

(iv) Sovereignty

Population

Population means People or citizens of the State. State presupposes citizenry i.e. Persons belonging to the state. State does make a distinction of US & THEM. State and its Laws have general bias towards its own people while the outsiders (Non-citizens) are endowed with certain disabilities. Though Non-citizens may be conferred certain rights, but their extent is generally limited when compared to those of Citizens. Further there may be rules by which a Non-citizen may be taken up as a Citizen and Citizen be regarded as non-citizen (e.g. if he takes up citizenship of another State). That is to say, although the State makes a distinction, the compartments are not always water-tight.

Land

Land means portion of Earth Surface. Every State must have a definitive territory i.e. Territorial limits to which it may exercise its authority. Although at times, there may be boundary disputes and authority may not be effectively exercised in remote regions, but one must be able to locate the State on the Globe.

Government

Government represents that part of the population which is bestowed with function of management of the affairs of the State. Its basic elements are

(i) Legislature – one that makes the laws

(ii) Executive – one that enforces the laws

(iii) Judiciary – one that interprets the law

Together, the three pillars form the government which look into the daily state affairs.

Sovereignty

Sovereignty is the idea of Supremacy over subjects. Austin has defined Sovereignty in terms - "If a determinate human superior, not in the habit of obedience to a like superior, receives habitual obedience from the bulk of a given society, that determinate Human Superior is Sovereign in that society, and that society (including the superior) is a society political and independent."

It is worth noting that the above definition was given in Monarchical times, hence the word Human superior is used. In modern democratic society, this human element need not be a physical human being like King or Queen, it can be Parliament, Constitution or even the People in general themselves under a common name or identity.

Once a village society develops into Political unit recognizing a village headman, similar to a Sovereign, and enforces its rules of conduct by virtue of power, a State is born.

2. LAW

Salmond has defined Law as the body of principles recognized and applied by the State in the administration of Justice. But this definition pertains to the domain of lawyers, judges and Courts.

Law, in common parlance, means rule. It signifies a rule of action, and is applied indiscriminately to all kinds of action, whether animate or inanimate, rational or irrational. It is in this sense terms such as Laws of Physics etc are used. In this sense, Law may be classified as -

Physical or Scientific Law

These are general principles expressing the regularity and harmony observable in the activities and operations of the universe. e.g. Earth revolves around the Sun.

Natural or Moral law

It is the principles of natural right and wrong, the principles of Natural Justice. It is the reason (sense of right and wrong, just and unjust) by which the world is governed. Cicero has pointed out that there is indeed a true law, right reason, agreeing with nature, diffused among all men, unchanging, everlasting……… It is not allowable to alter this law, nor to derogate from it, nor can it be repealed.

Imperative Law

It means any rule of action imposed upon men by some authority which enforces obedience to it.

Conventional Law

By Conventional law is meant any rule or system of rules agreed upon by persons for the regulation of their conduct towards each other.

Customary Law

It is any rule of action which is actually observed by men - any rule which is the expression of some actual uniformity of voluntary action. Custom is a law only for those who observe it.

Practical Law

Law which consists of rules for the attainment of some practical end may be termed as Practical law. e.g. Law of Health, Law of Style etc.

International Law

International Law or the law of Nations consists of those rules which govern Sovereign States in their relations and conduct towards each other.

Civil Law

This is the State authored law and our primary subject when the term law is used in reference to Justice as administered by Courts and legal procedures.

2.1. Administration of Justice

The administration of Justice may be defined as the maintenance of right within a political community by means of the physical force of the State.

The instrument of coercion employed by any regulative system is called a Sanction, and any rule of right supported by such means is said to be sanctioned. A Sanction is not necessarily a punishment or penalty. To punish wrongdoers is a very effectual way of maintaining the right, but it is not the only way. We enforce the rule of right, not only by increasing the thief, but by depriving him of his plunder, and restoring to its true owner, and each of these applications of the physical force of the State is equally a sanction.

Law is logically subsequent to administration of Justice. Courts of Justice are essentially Courts of law, justice in this usage being merely another name for Law. The administration of justice is essentially the enforcement of the law. The laws are the commands laid by the State upon it subjects and the law courts are the organs through which these commands are enforced.

But the administration of justice is perfectly possible without law at all. There is perfect possibility of Tribunals where Justice is not administered according to predetermined principles of Law, but according to unfettered discretion of Judge, in which equity and good conscience and natural justice are excluded by no rigid and artificial rules. Such Courts are Court of Justice and not of Law. Despite the above possibility, Law is desirable for the sake of clarity and impartiality.

3. RIGHTS & DUTIES

Before understanding the concept of Rights and Duties, we need to know what connotes "Wrong". The term "Wrong" is of common parlance and one often uses phrases such as I was wrong or the answer is wrong i.e. in sense of incorrectness of response. Largely, the term wrong is used in social form. In its legal sense, "Wrong" means contrary to Justice or Rule of right. It is also termed as legal injury i.e. An act classifies as "Wrong" (in legal parlance) if it results in Injury which the loss seeks to protect. If the Law does not recognise such injury or prescribe redress, the act is not a legal wrong, although it may be a moral or natural wrong.

A sense of wrong is one of emotional wrong, say for example, a boy proposes a girl who simply rejects the same. The boy may feel wronged, but the same does not qualify to be a legal one. On the contrary the proposal itself under certain circumstances qualify as voyeurism, which is a legal wrong.

Duty

Duty is an obligatory act. It is an act the opposite of which would be wrong. Breach of duty is a commission of wrong, or vice versa. A Duty is legal because it is legally recognized not necessarily because it is legally enforced or sanctioned.

Right

A Right is an interest recognized and protected by rule of right or law. It is an interest respect, for which is a duty, and the disregard of which is a wrong. If an act is right or just, it is so because and in so far as it promotes some form of Human interest. If any act is wrong or unjust, it is because the interest of men are prejudicially affected by it.

The above statement is very much relevant to legislative action. Justice is an abstract concept. The scale used to measure it is Law. So while drafting law/legislation, legislature is governed by the thought of Human interest. Here again, we can see although right is adjudged by Law, the source of Law itself is Right.

Since the interests of men conflict with each other, and it is impossible for all to receive rightful recognition, Rule of Justice selects some for protection and others are rejected. The interests which thus receive recognition and protection from the rules of right are called Rights. Rights and Duties are necessarily co-relative. A person's right is necessarily someone's duty.

Elements of legal right

A legal right has following five basic elements -

(a) Owner of right – Person in whom the right is vested.

(b) Subject of Duty – Person or persons against whom right avails and upon whom the co-relative duty lies.

(c) Content of Right – Act or omission which is obligatory on person.

(d) Object or Subject matter of Right – Thing to which act or omission relates.

(e) Title – Fact or event by the operation of which right became vested in its owner.

To understand this, take a simple example where A buys a piece of land from B. Here, A is the owner of right. The subject of duty is persons in general or world at large. The content of right is non-interference with A's exclusive use of land. Subject-matter of right is the said piece of land, and Title is the conveyance or the sale deed.

Thus every right involves three fold relation with the owner -

(a) It is right against some person or persons

(b) It is right to some act or omission of such person or persons

(c) It is right over or to something to which that act or omission relates

3.1. Legal Right in wider sense of the term

In wider and laxer sense, term "Right" includes any legally recognized interest whether it corresponds to a legal duty or not. In this generic sense, a legal right may be defined as any advantage or benefit which is in any manner conferred upon a person by rule of law. In this manner, Right can be classified as -

(i) Right (in strict sense)

(ii) Liberty

(iii) Power

(iv) Immunity

Liberty

Liberties are space provided by Law for free action, leaving the person to act according to his own conscience. They are the things which I may do without being restrained by the law. Liberties are the benefits which I derive from the the absence of legal duties imposed upon myself.

Although Right and Liberty may appear one, but take for example, A is owner of land. He has a right to exclusive use i.e. no one else can interfere with his possession and the same is the duty of Public at large. But it is his liberty to use or not. So, though his user right and liberty coincide, they are essentially different.

Power

Power may be defined as the ability conferred upon a person, by the law to determine by his own will directed to that end and the rights, duties, liabilities or other legal relations either of himself or other persons. Power resembles Liberties and differ from Rights in strict sense, in so much as they have no duties corresponding to them. A debt is not something as a right of action for its recovery. Former is a right in strict sense with corresponding duty of debtor to pay. Latter is legal power corresponding to liability of debtor.

Power is either ability to determine the legal relations of other persons i.e. authority or ability to determine one's own i.e capacity. In other words, Authority is power over others and Capacity is power over self.

Immunity

Immunity connotes exemption. It means an examination from enforcement of duty by the Court or State, thus disabling the person who otherwise would have a legal right.

Co-relatives

Right – Duty

Liberty – No Right

Power – Liability

Immunity – Disability

3.2. Right & Rights

Hear, a brief mention may be made of Right and Rights. Rights are one's individual interests enumerated in law, while Right connotes collection of all individual rights accrued to all persons. It is in this nature that we have rights but what the Law upholds is "Right" i.e. all rights collectively at the same time.

To add to this discussion, one may refer to Human Rights, those that are fundamental and germane to human life and cannot be alienated or forsaken. Indian constitution also enumerates them as Fundamental Rights. But the whole idea is of Human Right or Justice which we may recall is in its very nature abstract. Right are its limbs that we may feel or touch and define, but to define the whole is a task yet to be achieved.

4. BRANCHES OF LAW

Although, the law is one and whole in itself. It is not capable of disintegration or water-tight separation. But for the sake of lucidity, it is often classified as Private and Public.

Private law signifies rules that regulate the relationships between private individuals. It is a branch of the law that deals with the relations between individuals or institutions, rather than relations between them and the State. Private law includes law of contracts, law of torts, intellectual property rights, property law, family law, labour law.

Public law, on the other hand, is the part of law that governs relations between legal persons and a government, between different institutions within a state, between different branches of governments, as well as relationships between persons that are of direct concern to society. It also signifies principles that serve as a basis for the structure of the state and the relationships between the state and the citizens. Public Law includes constitutional law, administrative law, financial law, criminal law and procedural law, public international law.

It is pertinent to note that the distinction is more of form rather than of content. It depends upon the State as to what extent it seeks to recognise and protect the relations among various stakeholders. Say, for example, relation between master and servant is domain of labour law, but if the same acquires national importance, it may form part of public law also. Similarly, a single act may form tort as well as crime.

A brief description of some common branches of law is given below -

Public Law - Constitutional Law, Administrative Law, and Criminal Law.

Private Law - Law of Contract, Law of Torts, Family Law, and Property Law

4.1. Constitutional law

In general, Constitutional law forms the State and its elements. It regulates all legal relationships concerned with the state and law (separation of powers, essential features of the state, legislation). Constitutional law regulates the form of the public order and the administrative division of the territory; the status and role of the holder of the highest public authority, human rights; the primary elements of the public system (such as the parliament), their function, legal manner, structure, competence, and the basis and procedure of their formation (e.g. election procedure), as well as relations with the other elements of the public system (like the local government).

Due to its highest conclusive force, constitutional law also covers all constitutional legal provisions. Hence, constitutional law encompasses principles regulated by the constitution that are binding to each and every person. All the other law is subordinate to and derives its validity from the Constitutional Law.

4.2. Administrative law

Administrative law is Constitutional law in action. It regulates the activity of public authorities, their formation, powers, authority over and relationship with citizens, liability for violation etc.

The aim is to ensure the protection of public interests by providing legal framework within which the administration must act.

4.3. Civil law

Civil law forms the bulk of private law. Here, the term Civil Law, is used in a limited sense and not the whole body of Law. Here, it is used in reference to transactions of civil nature, giving rise to civil rights, wrongs and liabilities.

It can be divided into five parts: general part of civil law, family law, property law, law of succession and law of obligations. The general part of civil law is applicable as the general part of family and property law, law of succession, law of obligations, and the Commercial Code. It regulates persons (legal and natural persons), objects, transactions, representation, terms and due dates, enforcement and protection of civil rights. Family law regulates all relationships concerned with family and marriage (such as entering into a contract of marriage, the mutual obligations between spouses, obligations toward one's children, etc.). Law of succession covers matters such as succession, successors and bequeaths. Law of obligations regulates everything related to obligations that result in the liability to an act or omission on the part of one person to another. This obligation may arise out of Contract (Contractual Obligation) or otherwise (Tortious Obligation). Property law regulates real rights, their content, creation and extinguishment.

4.4. Criminal Law or Penal law

Criminal law is the body of law that relates to crime. It prescribes conduct perceived as threatening, harmful, or otherwise endangering to the property, health, safety, and moral welfare of people inclusive of one's self.

It dictates which actions are to be regarded as offences and prescribe punishments for them. Thereby, it determines the range of social relationships that stand under state protection and the violation of which results in punishment.

4.5. Procedural law

Procedural law determines the rules of court procedure. Procedural law establish hierarchy of courts, jurisdiction, method of hearing, rules of evidence, etc. The procedural law may be classified as civil or criminal, according to the nature of dispute and the remedy it proposes. Though procedural law is flexible and is often called hand maid of justice, but a significant violation of procedural rules may be a ground for nullification of proceedings.

CONSTITUTIONAL LAW

1. Introduction

Constitution is the founding stone for any Nation. It chalks out the element of State and its principles. The Indian constitution is a very unique document. Unlike, unwritten constitution of England, the Indian Constitution is well drafted. And unlike American Constitution, which is in its nature lays down broad principles, the Indian Constitution lays down principles in very specific manner with elaborate details, something which is unprecedented for any nation around the globe.

The salient features of the Indian constitution are as follows :-

1. It is Lengthiest written Constitution in the world.

2. It seeks a balance between Rigidity and Flexibility.

3. The Constitution establishes a Federal system of governance with unitary features.

4. It establishes Parliamentary form of Government, both at State and Union level.

5. The Constitution mandates for an Independent Judiciary, that is not dictated by the whims of the executive branch of the government.

6. Although, India has a federal structure, the Constitution lays down Single citizenship. That is, the citizens are citizens of India. There is nothing like State Citizenship (as in US), though domicile of State has been recognized.

7. The makers realized a need to incorporate Emergency provisions, to deal with certain situations that may arise.

1.1. Structure of Indian Constitution

Originally, The Indian Constitution consisted of 395 Articles divided into 22 parts, and 8 Schedules.

As on October 2021, the constitution has been amended 104 times, and presently it consists of 470 articles, which are grouped into 25 parts, with 12 schedules and five appendices.

The constitution begins with the Preamble, which is based on the objective resolution drafted and moved by Pt. Jawaharlal Nehru and adopted by constituent assembly. It is as follows:-

"We THE PEOPLE OF INDIA, having solemnly resolved to constitute India in to a SOVEREIGN SOCIALIST SECULAR DEMOCRATIC REPUBLIC and to secure to all its citizen:-

JUSTICE, social, Economic, and Political;

LIBERTY of thought, expression, belief, faith and worship;

EQUALITY of status and of opportunity;,

FRATERNITY assuring the dignity of the individual and the unity and integrity of the nation;

In our Constituent Assembly, this 26th November, 1949, do hereby adopt, enact and give to ourselves this constitution."

The preamble to the constitution is a key to open the minds of the makers and shows the general purpose for which they made the several provisions in the constitution. It discloses the source of the constitution, that is We The People. It sets out the goals which it seeks to achieve. Though, it neither grants nor lay prohibition on any power of the organs of government. Nonetheless, it is an important tool and is of extreme importance. The constitution should be read and interpreted in the light of grand and noble vision expressed in the preamble. Though, it is not justiciable i.e. not enforceable in courts of law. The Parliament may amend the preamble under article 368 of the constitution.

1.2. Influence of other constitutions

The makers of Indian Constitution had the opportunity to learn from the experiences of other nations. Thus, they have adopted many provisions from their Constitution. The following chart gives a glimpse on the said influence -

United Kingdom

(a) Parliamentary government

(b) Nominal/Titular head of the state

(c) The post of Prime Minister

(d) More powerful lower house

(e) Concept of single citizenship

(f) Legislative procedure

(g) Bicameral legislature

(h) Rule of law

(i) Cabinet form of Government

(j) Speaker of the legislature

(k) Prerogative writs

(l) Parliamentary privilege

United States

(a) Bill of Rights (Fundamental rights)

(b) Written constitution

(c) Preamble to the Constitution

(d) Federal structure of government

(e) Impeachment of the President

(f) The Post and role of the Vice President

(g) The institution of Supreme Court

(h) Removal of Supreme Court and High Courts Judges.

(i) Electoral College

(j) Independent judiciary and separation of powers

(k) Judicial review

(l) President as commander-in-chief of the armed forces

(n) Equal protection under law.

Ireland

(a) Directive principles of State Policy

(b) Nomination of members to the Rajya Sabha by the President

(c) Method of election of the President.

Australia

(a) Freedom of trade between states.

(b) National legislative power to implement treaties, even on matters outside normal federal jurisdiction.

(c) Concurrent List

(d) Provision of Joint Session of the Parliament

(e) Preamble terminology

France

(a) The ideals of Liberty, Equality, Fraternity in the Preamble.

(b) The ideals of Republic in the preamble.

Canada

(a) Quasi-federal government—a federal system with a strong central government

(b) Distribution of powers between the central and state

(c) Residual powers of the central government.

(d) Appointment of Governor of states by Centre.

(e) Advisory Jurisdiction of the Supreme Court.

Soviet Union

(a) Fundamental Duties under article 51-A.

(b) Planning Commission

(c) Ideals of justice (social, economic and political) in the Preamble

Weimar Republic / Germany

(a) Suspension of Fundamental rights during emergency.

South Africa

(a) Amendment procedure of the constitution.

(b) Election of the member of Rajya Sabha.

Japan

(a) Procedure established by Law

(b) Laws on which Supreme Court functions

2. NATURE OF INDIAN CONSTITUTION

Traditionally, a constitution is classified as unitary or federal. A Unitary Constitution is one where the powers of government are centralized in one government viz, the central government. The provinces are subordinate to the centre.

In a federal constitution, there is a division of powers between the federal and the state governments and both are independent in their own spheres.

Per Dr. K.C. Wheare – "Federalism means the method of dividing powers, so that the general and regional governments are each within a sphere coordinate and independent. Both the federal and the regional governments are coordinate and independent in their spheres and not sub-ordinate to one another".

The American Constitution is universally regarded as an example of federal constitution. It establishes dual policy or dual form of government that is the federal and the state governments. The power of both the central and state governments are divided and both are independent in their own spheres. The existence of co-ordinate authorities independence of each other is the gist of federal principles.

The framers of Indian Constitution attempted to avoid the difficulties faced by the federal constitution of U.S.A., Canada and Australia and incorporated certain unique features suited to the Indian conditions. Indian Constitution is often regarded as Quasi-federal, or a combination of both unitary and federal.

The reason for such a disposition is the power of Central Government to intervene in the affairs of State, in certain contingencies. But, the contingencies only point towards the foresight of the makers to run a federal system in more effective manner. The idea was never to form a federal system in traditional sense of the term, but a federal system that caters to the Indian needs, particularly those emerged at the time of Independence.

The constituent Assembly being aware that notwithstanding a common cultural heritage without political unity the country would disintegrate under the pressure of various forces therefore it addressed itself to the immensely complex task of devising a union with a strong centre. Article 1 says that – India, that is Bharat, shall be a Union of States. The constitution has postulated India as Union of states. Thus, the existence of federal structure of governance is a sine qua non for the Union.

Dr. Ambedkar, the Chief architect of the constitution observed that – the use of word Union is deliberate. The drafting committee wanted to make it clear that though the Idea was to be a federation, the federation was not a result of an agreement by the states to join in the federation and that federation not being the result of an agreement no state has right to separate from it. Though the country and the people may be divided into different states for convenience of administration the whole country is one integral whole.

3. TERRITORY

India is a union of states. The territory of Indian comprises of the territories of the States, and the Union territories as specified in the First Schedule. Further, it includes such other territories as may be acquired.

Parliament has been empowered to admit into the Union, or establish, new States by law. Parliament, by law, may also, form a new State by separation of territory from any State or by uniting two or more States or parts of States or by uniting any territory to a part of any State; increase the area of any State; diminish the area of any State; alter the boundaries of any State; alter the name of any State.

The Indian Constitution empowers the parliament to alter the territory or names, etc. of the State without their consent or concurrence. Such alteration may be made by law passed by simple majority. Thus, the very existence of a state depends upon the sweet will of the central government.

Parliament may by law increase or diminish the area of any state but it cannot cede Indian territory to a foreign state. Such an act can be implemented only by means of amendment of the constitution under Art. 368.

4. CITIZENSHIP

Citizenship represents the relation between the State (Nation) and its subject. It is a relationship between an individual and a state to which the individual owes allegiance and in turn is entitled to its protection. It is what distinguishes the subjects from non-citizens. It is a special status of an individual which accords him certain privileges and subject him to certain duties, which are otherwise inapplicable. For example, as a general rule only a citizen has the right to vote, the right to hold government offices. The law of a State may allow legitimate aliens to own property, carry on business, and attend religious or educational institutions. It may provide for protection of law and access to Law courts. But there shall be found certain distinguishing factors in all cases.

4.1. Acquisition of Citizenship

Under the Indian Constitution and Citizenship Act, a person may acquire Indian citizenship in following modes -

(i) Birth

(ii) Descent

(iii) Marriage

(iv) Naturalization

(v) Grant by Central Government

(vi) Acquisition of Territory

4.2. End of Citizenship

A valid citizenship may come to an end by any of the following modes -

(i) Renunciation

(ii) Termination - Voluntary acquisition of citizenship of another Nation.

(iii) Deprivation - A Naturalized citizen may be deprived of his citizenship in any of the following cases -

(a) Fraud, false representation etc. in obtaining the Certificate of Registration or Naturalization;

(b) Disloyal towards the Indian Constitution;

(c) Unlawful trading or communicating with the enemy during war;

(d) Imprisonment in any foreign country for 2 years or above;

(e) Ordinarily resident outside India for over 7 years without registration in Consulate's office.

5. FUNDAMENTAL RIGHTS

Fundamental Rights are the rights guaranteed by the Part – III of the constitution. Owing to the experience of the struggle for freedom and the second world war, It was thought that no government should be allowed unlimited power over its subjects. It was deduced that there are certain inalienable rights necessary for dignified human life. Fundamental Rights protect the liberties and freedom of the citizens against any invasion by the state. They establish a rule of law and not of man. It prevents the establishment of authoritarian and dictatorial rule in the country. They impose a negative obligation on the state.

There are following 6 fundamental rights enshrined in the Indian constitution -

1. Right to Equality
2. Right to Freedom
3. Right against Exploitation
4. Right to Freedom of Religion
5. Cultural and Educational Rights
6. Right to Constitutional Remedies

6. RIGHT TO EQUALITY

Article 14 of the Constitution states that the State shall not deny to any person equality before the law or the equal protection of the laws within the territory of India. The law does not provide for an absolute equality, which is impossible to achieve, but uses two expressions:-

(i) Equality before the law; and

(ii) Equal Protection of the laws

Equality before law is British concept of equality. It implies absence of any special privilege by virtue of birth, caste, creed, race, colour etc. It means that among equals the law should be equal and should be equally administered, that like should be treated alike. It means that no man is above the law and that every person, whatever be his rank or conditions, is subject to the jurisdiction of ordinary courts.

Equal Protection of the Laws is the American concept. It mean that all persons similarly circumstanced shall be treated alike both in the privileges conferred and liabilities imposed by the law equal law should be applied to all in the same situation and there should be no discrimination between one person and another.

The use of word person denotes that the right is available to both citizens and non-citizens, to natural as well as legal persons. The right to equality further prohibits discrimination on the grounds of religion race, caste, sex or place of birth, or use of wells, tanks, roads, or access to shops, restaurants or places of public entertainment. It also provides for equality of opportunity in matters of public employment. Lastly, the right prohibits the practice of untouchability and the use of titles.

The Constitution forbids class legislation; it permits reasonable classification of persons, objects and transactions by the legislature for the purpose of achieving desired ends. But classification must not be arbitrary, artificial or evasive. It must be based on intelligible differentia and have nexus with object sought to be achieved.

The modern concept of equality is fairness in action. Equality and arbitrariness are sworn enemies. When an act is arbitrary, it is implicitly violative of the principle of equality enshrined in the constitution.

7. RIGHT TO FREEDOM

7.1. The Six Freedoms

Article 19 (i) of the Constitution provides for following six freedoms:-

(a) Freedom of speech and expression

(b) Freedom of Assembly

(c) Freedom to from Association

(d) Freedom of Movement

(e) Freedom to reside and settle

(f) Freedom of Profession, occupation, trade or business.

These six freedom are available only to the citizens. They are not absolute, but subject to reasonable restriction in form of Security of the State, Friendly relation with foreign states, Public order, Decency and Morality, Contempt of Court, Defamation, Incitement to an offence, Sovereignty and Integrity of India.

By way of several Judicial pronouncements, this right includes freedom of press, right to know (information), right to hoist National Flag.

7.2. Protection in respect of conviction for offences

Article 20(1) provides protection from Ex-post facto criminal laws. It states that - No person shall be convicted of any offence except for violation of a law in force at the time of the commission of the Act charged as an offence, nor be subjected to a penalty greater than that which might have been inflicted under the law in force at the time of the commission of the offence.

Article 20(2) provides protection against Double jeopardy. It states that - No person shall be prosecuted and punished for the same offence more than once. The protection under this clause is available only in proceedings before a court of law or a judicial tribunal, and not in any proceedings before departmental or administrative authorities.

Article 20(3) gives protection from Self -Incrimination. It states that - No person accused of any offence shall be compelled to be a witness against himself. It extends to both oral and documentary evidence. It extends to only criminal proceedings and not to civil proceedings.

7.3. Right to Life & Personal Liberty

Article 21 states that - No person shall be deprived of his life or personal liberty except according to Procedure established by law.

The Supreme Court has given the widest possible interpretation of Life and Personal liberty. It is not merely animal existence. But the right has been interpret to include Right to Food, Livelihood, Shelter Privacy, Health &

Medical Assistance, Travel Abroad, Free Legal Aid, Speedy Trial, Pollution free Environment, Education, and also Right to die when terminally ill or in vegetative state.

To deprive a person of his Life or Liberty, the following Conditions must be fulfilled -

(i) There must me a valid law.

(ii) The law must provide a Procedure.

(iii) The Procedure must be Just, Fair and Reasonable

7.4. Right to Education

Article 21A declares that state shall provide free and compulsory education to all children of the age of six to fourteen years in such a manner as the state may decide. This provision makes only elementary education a fundamental right and not higher or professional education.

7.5. Protection against arrest and detention

Article 22 grants protection to persons who are arrested or detained. In general, a citizen has a right to be informed of the grounds of arrest, to consult and be defended by a legal practitioner. Further, he must be produced before a magistrate within 24 hours of arrest, excluding the journey time. But this right is unavailable to a person arrested under preventive detention law.

Where a person is detained under the preventive detention law, his detention cannot exceed three months unless an advisory board reports sufficient cause for extended detention. The grounds of detention should be communicated to the detenue, and he should be afforded an opportunity to make representation against the detention order.

8. RIGHT AGAINST EXPLOITATION

Article 23 prohibits traffic in human beings and other similar forms of forced labour. This right is available to both citizens and non-citizens. It protects the individual not only against state but also against the private person. However, the state may impose compulsory service for public purpose i.e military or social service.

Article 24 prohibits the employment of children below the age of 14 years in any factory, mine or other hazardous activities. Though they may be employed in work of domestic nature.

9. RIGHT TO FREEDOM OF RELIGION

Article 25 grants freedom of religion to all persons. It grants following freedoms -

(a) Freedom of conscience

(b) Right to profess

(c) Right to propagate

(d) Right to practice any religion

It applies to both religious beliefs and practices. The right is available to both citizen as well as non-citizens.

Article 26 provides that every religious denomination or any of its section shall have the following rights -

(a) to establish and maintain institutions for religious and charitable purposes;

(b) to manage its own affairs in matters of religion.

(c) to own and acquire movable and immovable property; and

(d) to administer such property in accordance with law.

Religious denomination refer to a body of individuals having a system of beliefs and a distinctive name. Ramakrishna mission, Anand Marg and Arvindo Society are not the denomination.

Article 27 lays down that no person shall be compelled to pay any taxes for the promotion or maintenance of any particular religion or religious denomination. That is, the state shall not spend the public money for the promotion or maintenance of any particular religion.

Article 28 provides that no religious instruction shall be provided in any educational institution wholly maintained out of state funds. However, this provision is inapplicable to educational institutions administered by the state but established under any endowment or trust requiring imparting of religious institution in such institution.

10. CULTURAL & EDUCATIONAL RIGHTS

Article 29 provides for the protection of interests of minorities. It provides that any section of the citizens residing in India having a distinct language, script or culture of its own shall have the right to conserve the same.

Further, article 30 provides that these linguistic and cultural (religious) minorities have a right to establish and administer educational institutions of their choice.

Minority educational institutions are of three types:-

1. Recognized and aided by the State.

2. Only recognized. but not aided.

3. Neither recognized. nor aided.

In view of article 30, only first two types of institutions are subject to state control.

11. RIGHT TO CONSTITUTIONAL REMEDIES

Right without remedy (enforcement) is meaningless. The constitution-makers have provided for an effective machinery for enforcement of fundamental rights. And this right of enforcement is itself a fundamental right. Dr. Ambedkar has called Article 32 as the soul of the constitution.

Article 32 empowers the Supreme Court to act as defender and guarantor of the fundamental rights of the citizen. Violation of fundamental right is sine qua non for applicability of article 32. Its purpose is to provide a guaranteed, effective, expeditious, inexpensive and summary remedy for the protection of the fundamental rights. Supreme Court has original and extensive powers for the same. It can issue writs in form of – Habeas Corpus, Mandamus, Certiorari, Prohibition, Quo-Warranto.

11.1. Habeas Corpus

Habeas Corpus is a Latin term which means to have the body of. It is a direction to produce the body of any person detained. The court examines the cause and legality of the detention. The person is set at liberty, if the detention is illegal. Thus writ is a bulwark of individual liberty against arbitrary detention. It can also be issued against private individual.

11.2. Mandamus

Mandamus literally means we command. It is command issued by the court to a public official asking him to perform his official duties that he has failed or refused to perform. It cannot be issued against a private individual or against the President or Governor or when the duty is discretionary.

11.3. Prohibition

Prohibition literally means to forbid. It is issued by higher court to a subordinate court or tribunal to prevent the latter from exceeding the jurisdiction.

11.4. Certiorari

Certiorari means to be certified. It is issued by higher court to a subordinate court or tribunal to quash an passed in excess of jurisdiction or there is a manifest error of law.

It is often said that Prohibition is prevention, Certiorari is the Cure. Prohibition restricts a tribunal from passing an illegal order, Certiorari rectifies any order so passed.

11.5. Quo-Warranto

Quo-Warranto literally means with what authority. It is issued by the court to inquire in to the legality of claim of a person to a public office.

12. DIRECTIVE PRINCIPLES OF STATE POLICY

Directive Principles of State Policy or D.P.S.P. (as they are popularly called) are contained in Part IV of the Constitution. DPSP consists of all the ideals which the State should follow and keep in mind while formulating policies and enacting laws for the country.

The main object in enacting the directive principles is to set standard of achievement before the legislature and the executive, and other authorities, as a measure of their success.

The following chart gives a glimpse of the directive contained in the Constitution -

Article 38 – Promotion of welfare of the people by securing a social order by ensuring social, economic and political justice.

Article 39 – Right to an adequate means of livelihood, Ownership and control of resources to serve the common good, Avoid concentration of wealth, Equal pay for equal work for men and women.

Article 39A – Equal Justice and Free legal aid.

Article 40 – Organization of Village Panchayats.

Article 41 – Right to work, to education and to public assistance.

Article 42 – Just and humane conditions of work and maternity benefit.

Article 43 – Living wage and decent standard of life.

Article 43A – Participation of workers in management of industries.

Article 43B – Promotion of cooperative societies.

Article 44 – Uniform civil code for citizens.

Article 45 – Early childhood care.

Article 46 – Promotion of educational and economic interests of the weaker sections.

Article 47 – Raise level of nutrition and improve public health.

Article 48 – Organize agriculture and animal husbandry.

Article 48A – Protection and improvement of environment and safeguarding of forests and wild life.

Article 49 – Protection of monuments and places of National importance.

Article 50 – Separation of Judiciary from Executive.

Article 51 – Promotion of international peace and security, and friendly relations among Nations.

13. RELATIONSHIP BETWEEN FUNDAMENTAL RIGHTS & DIRECTIVE PRINCIPLES

Fundamental Rights are justiciable rights, while DPSP are mere guidelines for the State to be followed. They cannot be enforced by way of writ or otherwise by the Constitutional Courts. Fundamental Rights are individual freedoms, while DPSP are meant for larger social good. At a glance, they may look contradictory to each other.

In Keshavananda Bharti v. State of Kerala, The Supreme Court held that the aim of fundamental rights & D.P.S.P. is to bring about a social revolution and establish a welfare state. That they should be interpreted and applied together in a harmonious manner.

14. FUNDAMENTAL DUTIES

Article 51A of the Constitution lays down the following fundamental duties of every Indian Citizen -

(a) to abide by the Constitution and respect its ideals and institutions, the National Flag and the National Anthem;

(b) to cherish and follow the noble ideals which inspired our national struggle for freedom;

(c) to uphold and protect the sovereignty, unity and integrity of India;

(d) to defend the country and render national service when called upon to do so;

(e) to promote harmony and the spirit of common brotherhood amongst all the people of India transcending religious, linguistic and regional or sectional diversities; to renounce practices derogatory to the dignity of women;

(f) to value and preserve the rich heritage of our composite culture;

(g) to protect and improve the natural environment including forests, lakes, rivers and wild life, and to have compassion for living creatures;

(h) to develop the scientific temper, humanism and the spirit of inquiry and reform;

(i) to safeguard public property and to abjure violence;

(j) to strive towards excellence in all spheres of individual and collective activity so that the nation constantly rises to higher levels of endeavour and achievement;

(k) who is a parent or guardian to provide opportunities for education to his child or, as the case may be, ward between the age of six and fourteen years.

15. UNION EXECUTIVE

15.1. The President

Article 52 provides that there shall be a President of India. Article 53 states that the executive power of the Union shall vest in the President. He is also the Supreme Command of the Defence Forces of the Union. Since the Constitution envisages Rule of Law and not of Man, the President may exercise the Union's executive power only in accordance with the Constitution.

Election of President

The President is elected by the members of an electoral college consisting of the elected members of both Houses of Parliament and the elected members of the Legislative Assemblies of the States (including Union Territories).

The manner of election is system of proportional representation by means of single transferable vote. The voting is done by secret ballot. The term of office is Five years from the date the President enters upon his office. He may resign from his office by resignation addressed to the Vice-President, who shall communicate it to the Speaker of Lok Sabha.

The President may be impeached for violation of the Constitution. When a charge has been preferred by either House of Parliament, the other House shall investigate the charge or cause the charge to be investigated and the President shall have the right to appear and to be represented at such investigation.

Executive Power of the Union

Article 73 provides that the executive power of the Union extends to all matters set out in the Union List in Seventh Schedule of the Constitution, and to the exercise of such rights, authority and jurisdiction as are exercisable by the Government of India by virtue of any treaty or agreement.

15.2. The Vice-President

Article 63 of the Constitution provides for a Vice-President of India. He is also the ex-officio Chairman of the Council of States (Rajya Sabha). The Vice-President acts as the President and discharges his functions during casual vacancies in the office.

15.3. Council of Ministers

Article 74 of the Constitution provides for a Council of Ministers with the Prime Minister as their head to aid and advise the President, who is required to act in accordance with their advice in the exercise of the presidential functions. The President may, however, require the Council of Ministers to reconsider such advice, either generally or otherwise; once the Council of Ministers have reconsidered their advice and tendered it to the President, the President is bound to act in accordance with it.

The Prime Minister is appointed by the President and the other Ministers are appointed by the President on the advice of the Prime Minister. The ministers are individually responsible to the President, while the Council is collectively responsible to the House of the People (Lok Sabha).

15.4. Attorney-General

Article 76 of the Constitution provides that the President shall appoint a person qualified to be Judge of the Supreme Court to be Attorney-General of India. He is required to advise the Government of India upon such legal matters, and to perform such other duties of a legal character, as may be referred or assigned to him by the President, and to discharge the functions conferred on him by the Constitution, or any other law for the time being in force.

16. STATE EXECUTIVE

16.1. The Governor

Article 153 of the Constitution provides that each State shall have a Governor, appointed by the President, and in whom the executive power of the State vests. The powers and functions of a Governor of a State are comparable to that of the President in relation to the Union.

The Governor acts on the advice of the Council of Ministers of the State, except in so far as he is by or under this constitution required to exercise his functions or any of them in his discretion. The Governor's discretion as to whether or not he may act in his own discretion, or only upon the advice of the Council of Ministers in a particular matter, is final.

Executive Power of the State

Article 164 of the Constitution provides that the executive power of a State extends to those matters in respect of which the Legislature of a State has the authority to make laws, that is matters in State List and Concurrent List. However, in respect of matters in the Concurrent List, this power is subject to the executive power expressly conferred by the Constitution or by any law made by Parliament upon the Union.

16.2. Council of Ministers

Similar to the Union, the Chief Minister of a State is appointed by the Governor, and the other Ministers are appointed by the Governor on the advice of the Chief Minister. The Chief Minister and the other Ministers hold office during the pleasure of the Governor, and the Council of Ministers of a State is collectively responsible to the Legislative Assembly of the State.

16.3. Advocate-General

Article 165 of the Constitution provides that there shall be an Advocate-General for each State. The functions of an Advocate-General in relation to the Governor and the State are analogous to those of the Attorney-General in relation to the President and the Union.

17. THE UNION LEGISLATURE - PARLIAMENT

17.1. The Parliament

The Parliament of India consists of the President, and two Houses, known as the Council of States (Rajya Sabha), and the House of the People (Lok Sabha).

17.2. Council of States

The Council of States has 250 members, of whom 12 are nominated by the President, and 238 are elected representatives of the States and Union Territories. The representatives of the States are elected by the elected members of the Legislative Assembly of the State through the system of proportional representation, using a single transferable vote.

The Council of States is a permanent body, with one-third of its members retiring and being replaced by new members every second year.

The Vice-President is the ex-officio Chairman of the Rajya Sabha. A Deputy Chairman is elected by the members from among themselves.

17.3. House of the People

The House of the People consists of not more than 530 members elected directly by the voters in the States, not more than 20 members to represent the Union Territories, chosen in the manner provided under law, and not more than two members belonging to the Anglo-Indian community are nominated by the President.

The House of the People continues for five years from the date appointed for its first meeting. A Speaker and a Deputy Speaker is elected by the members from among themselves.

17.4. Meetings of the Parliament

The President summons each House of Parliament from time to time, and may prorogue each or both the Houses, and may dissolve the House of the People. There should not be an interval of more than six months between the sessions of the Houses of Parliament.

Members of Parliament enjoy freedom of speech in the House. No member is liable to any proceedings in any court in respect of anything said or any vote given by him in Parliament, and no person would be so liable in respect of the publication by or under the authority of either House of Parliament of any report, paper, votes, or proceedings.

Passing of Bills

A Bill, except Money Bill, may be introduced in either House of Parliament. A Bill is deemed to be passed only when both Houses of Parliament have passed it.

The President may call for a joint sitting of both Houses if a Bill is passed in one House but rejected in the other; if the Houses have finally disagreed as to the amendments to be made in the Bill; or if more than six months have elapsed from the date that a Bill, having been passed by one House, has been received in the other House without its passing the Bill.

Lok Sabha has monopolistic power over Money Bills. A Money Bill may be introduced only in Lok Sabha. Once passed by Lok Sabha, it is transmitted to Rajya Sabha for its recommendations within 14 days. Lok Sabha may thereupon either accept or reject all or any of the recommendations of Rajya Sabha. If Lok Sabha does not accept recommendations or Bill is not returned within 14 days, Bill is deemed to have been passed by both the Houses in the form in which it was passed by Lok Sabha.

After a Bill is passed by the Houses of Parliament, it is presented to the President, who may either assent to it or withhold assent. If the President withholds assent, he must return the Bill for reconsideration and may also propose amendments. The Houses may or may not accept such recommendations or amendments, and send the Bill again to the President, who cannot now withhold assent.

17.5. Legislative Powers of the President

The President has been empowered to promulgate Ordinances. If at any time, except when both Houses of Parliament are in session, the President is satisfied that circumstances exist which render it necessary for him to take immediate action, he may promulgate such Ordinances as the circumstances appear to him to require. An Ordinance so promulgated has the same force and effect as an Act of Parliament.

Such Ordinance is laid before the Parliament, and would cease to operate six weeks after the reassembly of Parliament, or if both Houses pass resolutions disapproving the Ordinance within the six weeks. The President may also withdraw the Ordinance at any time.

18. THE STATE LEGISLATURE

Each State has a Legislature, comprising the Governor and a Legislative Assembly (Vidhan Sabha), and, in some States, a Legislative Council (Vidhan Parishad).

Members of the Legislative Assembly are directly elected, and the members of the Legislative Councils are appointed through a combination of indirect election, and nomination by the Governor.

The Legislative Assembly of a State, unless sooner dissolved, continues for five years from the date appointed for its first meeting. The Governor summons the House or Houses of the Legislature of a State to meet from time to time, provided that not more than six months should intervene between meetings of the Houses. The Governor also has the authority to prorogue either or both the Houses, and to dissolve the Legislative Assembly.

Similar to Parliament, there is a Speaker and a Deputy Speaker of the Legislative Assembly, and a Chairman and Deputy Chairman of the Legislative Council in each State.

The legislate procedure of the State Assemblies is similar to that of Parliament. In Bicameral Legislature, a Bill (except Money Bill) may be introduced in either House of the Legislature, and both Houses must agree on a Bill before it is deemed to have been passed.

When the Legislature of a State passes a Bill, it is sent to the Governor for assent. The Governor may either assent to the Bill, withhold assent, or reserve the Bill for the consideration of the President. If the Governor withholds assent, the Governor must, as soon as possible, return the Bill if it is not a Money Bill, to the Legislature, and ask that the Legislature reconsider the Bill, along with any suggested amendments. If the Legislature sends the Bill back to the Governor with or without the suggested amendments, the Governor may not withhold assent any further. The Governor must reserve for the consideration of the President any Bill which, in the Governor's opinion, would, if it became law, derogate from the powers of the High Court and endanger its Constitutional position.

18.1. Legislative Power of the Governor

At any time except when the Legislature of a State is in session, if the Governor is satisfied that circumstances exist that make it necessary for her to take immediate action, the Governor may promulgate such Ordinances as the circumstances appear to him to require. Any Ordinance promulgated by the Governor must be presented before the Legislature as soon as it is in session, and expires six weeks from the reassembly of the Legislature, or earlier, if the Legislature passes a resolution disapproving it.

19. THE UNION JUDICIARY

Article 124 of the Constitution provides that there shall be a Supreme Court of India, consisting of a Chief Justice and such number of other judges as the Parliament may by law prescribe. All judges of the Supreme Court are appointed by the President upon consultation with such judges of the Supreme Court and the High Courts as the President deems necessary.

19.1. Qualifications

A person shall not be qualified for appointment as a Judge of the Supreme Court unless he is a citizen of India and

(a) has been a Judge of High Court for at least five years; or

(b) has been an advocate of High Court for at least ten years; or

(c) is, in the opinion of the President, a distinguished jurist.

19.2. Tenure

Judges of the Supreme Court hold office until the age of sixty-five years. He may resign from office. A Judge of Supreme Court may only be removed on the ground of 'proved misbehaviour or incapacity' by an order of the President, passed after an address by each House of Parliament, supported by special majority in the same session.

19.3. Court of Record

The Supreme Court is a court of record. That its acts and judicial proceedings are recorded for perpetual memory and testimony, and that it has the authority to punish for its own contempt.

19.4. Jurisdiction of the Supreme Court

Original Jurisdiction

The Supreme Court has exclusive and original jurisdiction over any disputes:

(a) between the Government of India and one or more States, or

(b) between the Government of India and any State or States on one side, and one or more States on the other side, or

(c) between two or more States,

Appellate Jurisdiction

An appeal will lie to the Supreme Court from any judgment, decree, or final order of a High Court, whether in a civil, criminal, or other proceeding, if the High Court certifies under Article 134-A that the case involves a substantial question of law as to the interpretation of the Constitution.

In Civil proceedings, an appeal lies to the Supreme Court from any judgment, decree or final order of a High Court if the High Court certifies under Article134-A that -

(a) that the case involves a substantial question of law of general importance; and

(b) that in the opinion of the High Court the said question needs to be decided by the Supreme Court.

In criminal proceedings, an appeal lies to the Supreme Court from any judgment, final order, or sentence of a High Court, if the High Court -

(a) has on appeal reversed an order of acquittal of an accused person and sentenced him to death; or

(b) has withdrawn for trial before itself any case from any court subordinate to its authority and has in such trial convicted the accused person and sentenced him to death; or

(c) certifies under article 134A that the case is a fit one for appeal to the Supreme Court.

Special Leave Petition

Article 136 of the Constitution provides that the Supreme Court may, in its discretion, grant special leave to appeal from any judgment, decree, determination, sentence or order in any cause or matter passed or made by any court or tribunal in the territory of India. However, this discretion does not extend to any judgment or order of Armed Forces tribunal.

Power of Review

The Supreme Court has the power to review any judgment pronounced or order made by it, subject to the law made by Parliament. Review includes curative petitions as well.

19.5. Other Important Provisions as to the Supreme Court

The law declared by the Supreme Court is binding on all courts within the territory of India. However, the Supreme Court is not bound by its own decisions. It may overrule its previous decisions but a decision of a bench is binding upon a smaller or co-ordinate bench. The smaller or equal bench may request that a matter be placed before a larger bench.

The Supreme Court in the exercise of its jurisdiction may pass such decree or make such order as is necessary for doing complete justice in any cause or matter pending before it, and any decree so passed or order so made shall be enforceable throughout the territory of India.

The President may also refer a question to the Supreme Court for consideration if it appears to the President that a question of law or fact has arisen, or is likely to arise, which is of such a nature and of such public importance that it is necessary to obtain the Supreme Court's opinion upon it.

20. THE HIGH COURTS IN THE STATES

Article 214 provides that there shall be a High Court for each State. Judge of a High Court is appointed by the President by warrant under his hand and seal after consultation with the Chief Justice of India and the Governor of the State. In the case of appointment of a Judge other than the Chief Justice, the Chief Justice of the High Court is also consulted.

20.1. Qualifications

A person shall not be qualified for appointment as a Judge of a High Court unless he is a citizen of India and -

(a) has for at least ten years held a judicial office in the territory of India; or

(b) has for at least ten years been an advocate of a High Court.

20.2. Tenure

Judges of the High Court hold office until the age of sixty-two years. He may resign from office. A Judge of High Court may only be removed on the ground of 'proved misbehaviour or incapacity' by an order of the President, passed after an address by each House of Parliament, supported by special majority in the same session.

20.3. Court of Record

The High Court is a court of record. That its acts and judicial proceedings are recorded for perpetual memory and testimony, and that it has the authority to punish for its own contempt.

20.4. Power of High Court to issue Writs

Article 226 states that every High Court shall have power, throughout the territories in relation to which it exercises jurisdiction, to issue to any person, or authority, including in appropriate cases, any Government, within those territories directions, orders or writs, including writs in the nature of habeas corpus, mandamus, prohibition, quo warranto and certiorari or any of them, for the enforcement of any of the rights conferred by Part III (Fundamental Rights) and for any other purpose. For any other purpose means enforcement of legal rights (other than fundamental rights).

Further the article 226 provides that High Court may issue directions, orders, or writs to any Government, authority or person if the cause of action, wholly or in part, arises within the territorial jurisdiction of that High Court, notwithstanding that the seat of such Government or authority or residence of that person is not within the territorial jurisdiction of that High Court.

The remedy under A.226 is a discretionary remedy. As such, the High Court has the discretion to refuse the grant of Writ remedy if it is satisfied that the aggrieved party has an effective alternate remedy. The High Court is also empowered to grant interim relief in appropriate cases.

20.5. Power of Superintendence over all courts

Article 227 confers on all High Courts the power of superintendence over all courts and tribunals throughout its territorial jurisdiction. This power is of an administrative as well as a judicial nature.

The High Court may-

(a) call for returns from such courts;

(b) make and issue general rules and prescribe forms for regulating the practice and proceedings of such courts;

(c) prescribe forms in which books, entries and accounts shall be kept by the officers of any such courts.

21. THE UNION TERRITORIES

Apart from the States, there are several Union Territories (UT). Every Union Territory is administered by the President, acting, to the extent that the President thinks fit, through an administrator appointed by the President with such designation as the President may specify.

When a Governor of a State is appointed as an administrator of a Union Territory, he acts independently of the Council of Ministers in respect of UT's administration.

UT's are centrally administered, but they are not merged with the Central Government and maintain their distinct constitutional identity.

UT of Delhi and Pondicherry also have Legislative Assemblies, similar to State Legislature.

22. LOCAL SELF GOVERNMENT

Having regard to India's vast land area and diversity in culture, there was a need for a local body to administer day to day affairs at the root level. With greater Urbanization over the years, there was a greater demand for a more sophisticated form of local self government.

To this end, Part IX, IX-A, and X of the Constitution provide for establishment of Panchayats for Rural Areas, Municipalities for Metropolitan and Municipal Areas, and a Scheme of Administration for Scheduled and Tribal Areas.

23. CENTRE – STATE RELATIONSHIP

Part XI of the Constitution lays down the Legislative and Administrative Relationship between the Union of India and the States

23.1. Legislative Relationship

The Constitution, in Schedule VII, has classified areas or subjects into three categories, namely – Union List, State List and Concurrent List.

Union List enumerates subjects of National importance that require uniformity throughout the Nation. Parliament alone has the authority to make laws on these subject matters for whole or any part of the territory of India. Also, No law made by Parliament can be deemed invalid on the ground that it has extra-territorial operation.

State List enumerates subjects of local importance that need flexibility or are needed to be dealt with keeping in mind the peculiar situation of the State. State Legislature cannot make a law having extra-territorial operation, but where a law made by State Legislature has sufficient nexus between the State and the subject-matter, the same is valid.

Concurrent List enumerates subjects of National importance but may require flexibility at the level of State.

Parliament but not State Legislature has power to legislate on residuary subject matters, not enumerated in any of the three lists.

If a law deals with a subject in one List, but also touches upon a subject in another List, over which Parliament/Legislature does not have legislative competence, the true character and nature of the legislation has to be ascertained. If, upon examination, it is found that the legislation is in substance on a matter assigned to the legislature enacting the statute, then it must be held valid in its entirety even though it may incidentally tread upon matters beyond its competence. This is termed as the Doctrine of pith and substance.

Parliament's Power to Legislate on State Subjects

Parliament is empowered to legislate on subjects in the State List in following circumstances -

(a) When Council of States passes a resolution with special majority that it is necessary or expedient in the national interest for Parliament to legislate on State subject. (A. 249)

(b) When a proclamation of Emergency is in operation (A. 250),

(c) When two or more States pass a resolution to that effect (A. 252).

(d) To give effect to international agreements. (A.253)

Effect of Inconsistency or Repugnancy (A.254)

If a provision of any law made by a State Legislature is repugnant to any law made by Parliament that Parliament is competent to enact, then the law made by the State Legislature would be invalid to the extent of the repugnancy.

Where a law made by State Legislature on subject of Concurrent List contains any provision repugnant to the provisions of law made by Parliament, then, the law so made by the Legislature of such State shall, if it has been reserved for the consideration of the President and has received his assent, prevail in the State.

In the latter situation, however, Parliament may pass a law at any time, adding to, amending, varying, or repealing the State law.

23.2. Administrative Relations

The executive power of State shall be exercised as to ensure compliance with the laws made by Parliament, and the executive power of the Union extends to the giving of such directions to a State as the Government of India deems necessary for that purpose.

The Union may also provide for the adjudication of disputes relating to the use, distribution, or control of the waters of, or in, any inter-State river or river valley.

The President may also establish Inter-State Council to inquire into and advise upon inter-State disputes, and make recommendations for better coordination.

24. FINANCE

Article 265 of the Constitution states that No tax shall be levied or collected except by authority of law. It makes clear that a tax may only be imposed under statutory law, enacted by a legislature that has the competence to pass a law on the subject concerned. No tax can be imposed by executive order.

All revenues raised by the Government of India, as well as all moneys received, are to be formed into the Consolidated Fund of India. Similarly, all revenues raised and moneys received by a State Government are to be formed into a Consolidated Fund of that State. No moneys may be appropriated from the Consolidated Fund of India or from the Consolidated Fund of a State except in accordance with law, and for the purposes and manner provided in the Constitution.

The Constitution lays down elaborate provisions for imposition, collection and appropriation of taxes by the Centre and the States.

It is worth noting that a State may not impose tax on the sale or purchase of goods if such sale or purchase takes place outside the State, or in the course of the import of the goods into, or the export of the goods out of India.

25. PROPERTY, CONTRACT AND SUITS

25.1. Property & Contracts

All contracts made in the exercise of the executive power of the Union or of a State shall be expressed to be made by the President, or by the Governor of the State. All such contracts and assurances of property made in the exercise of that power shall be executed on behalf of the President or the Governor by such persons and in such manner as he may direct or authorize.

However, neither the President nor the Governor is personally liable in respect of such contracts or assurances of property, nor the persons who execute such contracts or assurances of property on behalf of the President or the Governor are personally liable thereof.

25.2. Obligations and Suits

Article 300 provides that the Government of India may sue or be sued by the name of the Union of India and the Government of a State may sue or be sued by the name of the State.

The liability of Government under a Contract is same as any legal person. While in torts, the Government cannot be held liable for acts committed by its servants in the exercise of its Sovereign functions.

25.3. Right to Property

Originally a fundamental right, the right to property has been reduced to a mere legal right the Forty-fourth Constitutional amendment. It states that No person shall be deprived of his property save by authority of law.

The effect of above constitutional amendment is that the executive cannot deprive a person of his property without the authority of law. 'Law' in this context means an Act of Parliament or a State Legislature, a rule, or a statutory order, having the force of law.

26. TRADE, COMMERCE AND INTERCOURSE

Article 301 states that subject to other provisions of Part XIII of the Constitution Trade, commerce and intercourse throughout the territory of India shall be free.

Trade and commerce, here, refers to only lawful trading activities. Activities against public policy, for example, gambling, are not accorded any protection.

However, Parliament may impose such restrictions on the freedom of trade, commerce or intercourse within the territory of India as may be necessary in the public interest. But Parliament may not discriminate between States through such restrictions, unless it is necessary to do so for the purpose of dealing with a situation arising from scarcity of goods in any part of the territory of India.

A State Legislature may by law impose tax on goods imported from other States or UTs. But such law cannot discriminate between goods imported and goods manufactured in the State.

It may also impose reasonable restrictions on the freedom of trade, commerce or intercourse with or within the State as may be required in the public interest. Such a law bill must be introduced only with the previous sanction of the President.

27. SERVICES UNDER THE UNION & STATES

The appropriate Legislature may regulate the recruitment, and conditions of service of persons appointed, to public services and posts in connection with the affairs of the Union or of any State.

The rules providing for the terms of service can be unilaterally altered by the Government. Once appointed to a post or office, a government servant acquires status, and the government servant's rights and obligations are no longer determined by the consent of both parties, but by statute or statutory rules, which may be framed and altered unilaterally by the Government. The legal position of a government servant is more of status than of contract.

27.1. Doctrine of Pleasure

Except as expressly provided by the constitution, every person who is a member of a defence service or of a civil service of the Union or of an all-India service or holds any post connected with defence or any civil post under the Union, holds office during the pleasure of the President, and every person who is a member of a civil service of a State or holds any civil post under a State holds office during the pleasure of the Governor of the State.

The importance of the 'doctrine of pleasure' recognized in Article 310 is that firstly, the Government has the right to regulate or determine the tenure of its employees at pleasure, without being restricted by any terms in their contract to the contrary; and secondly, that the Government has no power to restrict or give up its prerogative of terminating the services of its employees at pleasure under any contract with the employee.

27.2. Limitations on Doctrine of Pleasure

Firstly, no person who is a member of a civil service of the Union or an all-India service or a civil service of a State or holds a civil post under the Union or a State shall be dismissed or removed by an authority subordinate to that by which he was appointed.

Secondly, no such person as aforesaid shall be dismissed or removed or reduced in rank except after an inquiry in which he has been informed of the charges against him and given a reasonable opportunity of being heard in respect of those charges. Though, it is not necessary to give such person any opportunity of making a representation on the penalty proposed.

Further, holding of inquiry is not necessary in the following conditions -

(a) Where a person is dismissed or removed or reduced in rank on the ground of conduct which has led to his conviction on a criminal charge; or

(b) Where the authority empowered to dismiss or remove a person or to reduce him in rank is satisfied that for some reason, to be recorded by that authority in writing, it is not reasonably practicable to hold such inquiry; or

(c) Where the President or the Governor, as the case may be, is satisfied that in the interest of the security of the State it is not expedient to hold such inquiry.

It is pertinent to note that the above protection does not extend to an employee of a Government company incorporated under the Companies Act, not being a Government department. Also, the said protection is unavailable in the cases of compulsorily retirement in accordance with service rules.

27.3. Public Service Commission

The Constitution provides for establishment of a Public Service Commission for the Union and a Public Service Commission for each State.

The Chairman and Members of Union and State Commissions are appointed by the President and the Governor respectively. The Chairman and members have security of tenure. The Chairman or any other member of a Public Service Commission shall only be removed from his office by order of the President on the ground of misbehaviour after the Supreme Court, on reference being made to it by the President, has, on inquiry reported that the Chairman or member ought to be removed on any such ground.

28. TRIBUNALS

Article 323-A of the Constitution provides the Parliament an authority to create administrative tribunals for the adjudication or trial of disputes or complaints relating to the recruitment and conditions of service of any persons appointed to public services and posts in connection with the affairs of the Union or of any State, or of any local or other authority within the territory of India, or under the control of the Government of India, or of any corporation owned or controlled by the Government.

Article 323-B of the Constitution provides the appropriate Legislature an authority to provide for the adjudication or trail by tribunals of any disputes, complaints or offences with respect to matters like Tax, Foreign exchange, export-import, Industrial dispute, ceiling on urban property, Elections, Rent and tenancy, and other incidental matters.

Such law may provide for exclusion of jurisdiction of all courts except the Supreme Court and the High Courts.

29. ELECTIONS

The superintendence, direction and control of the preparation of the electoral rolls for, and the conduct of, all elections to Parliament, State Legislature, and offices of President and Vice-President under the constitution shall be vested in Election Commission.

The Election Commission shall consist of the Chief Election Commissioner and such number of other Election Commissioner as the President may from time to time fix.

Chief Election Commissioner shall not be removed from his office except in like manner and on the like grounds as a Judge of the Supreme Court. Election Commissioner or a Regional Commissioner shall not be removed from office except on the recommendation of the Chief Election Commissioner.

There shall be one general electoral roll for every territorial constituency for election to either House of Parliament or Legislature of a State. No discrimination on grounds only of religion, race, caste, sex is permissible in electoral role. Nor any special electoral roll be created only on the basis of religion, race, caste, sex or any of them.

The elections to the House of People and Legislative Assembly of State shall be on the basis of adult suffrage. Every person who is a citizen of India and who is not less than eighteen years of age and is not otherwise disqualified under the Constitution or any other law on the ground of non-residence, unsoundness of mind, crime or corrupt or illegal practice, shall be entitled to be registered as a voter.

30. EMERGENCY PROVISIONS

From the provisions of the Constitution, the emergency may be classified into – National, State and Financial.

30.1. National Emergency

If the President is satisfied that a grave emergency exists whereby the security of India or of any part of the territory thereof is threatened, whether by war or external aggression or armed rebellion, he may, by proclamation, make a declaration to that effect. Proclamation of Emergency may be varied or revoked by subsequent Proclamation. A Proclamation for National Emergency may be issued by the President only on written advice of the Union Cabinet.

Such Proclamation is initially effective for a period of one month. During this period, it must be laid before each House of Parliament. Only when each House approves the Proclamation with special majority, the same continues in force for a period of six months.

30.2. Effect of Proclamation of National Emergency

While a Proclamation of Emergency is in operation -

(a) the executive power of the Union shall extend to the giving of directions to any State as to the manner in which the executive power thereof is to be exercised; and

(b) the legislative power of the Parliament shall include power to make laws conferring powers and imposing duties upon the Union or its authorities, although that subject matter is not enumerated in the Union List.

(c) the Article 19, which provides for freedom of speech and expression and other freedoms becomes suspended.

(d) the President may by order declare that the right to move any court for the enforcement of fundamental rights except article 20 and 21, and all proceedings pending in any court for the enforcement of these rights shall remain suspended.

30.3. State Emergency

If, on receipt of a report from the Governor of a State or otherwise, the President is satisfied that a situation has arisen in which the government of the State cannot be carried out in accordance with the provisions of the Constitution, the President may by Proclamation -

(a) Assume the functions of State Government and powers vested in or exercisable by the Governor or any other authority in the State, other than the Legislature;

(b) Declare that the powers of State Legislature shall be exercisable by the Parliament; and

(c) Make such incidental or consequential provisions as the President thinks fit to give effect to the Proclamation.

However, the President is not authorised to assume the powers of a High Court.

The Proclamation for State Emergency must be laid before both the Houses of Parliament within two months. Where-after, the Proclamation may continue only with the approval of Parliament for a period of six months at a time, subject to a maximum of three years.

The exercise of the President's power under article 356 is subject to judicial review. Though the President's satisfaction is subjective, it has to be based on objective facts. If the power is exercised in a mala fide manner, it can be struck down. The President is obliged to produce the material on which the action =is based. While the Court cannot go into the correctness of the material or its adequacy, it can see whether it was relevant to the action. If the Court comes to the conclusion that the President's action was unconstitutional, it can restore the dismissed government to office, and revive and reactivate the Legislative Assembly, whether it was dissolved or kept under suspension.

30.4. Financial Emergency

If the President is satisfied that a situation has arisen whereby the financial stability or credit of India or of any part of the territory thereof is threatened, he may by a Proclamation make a declaration to that effect.

Such a Proclamation must be laid before each House of Parliament and shall cease to operate at the expiration of two months, unless before the expiration of that period it has been approved by resolutions of both Houses of Parliament.

During the period of Proclamation, the executive authority of the Union shall extend to giving of directions to any State to observe specified canons of financial propriety, and to giving of such other directions as the President may deem necessary and adequate for the purpose.

31. CONSTITUTIONAL AMENDMENT

Article 368 provides that Parliament may, in the exercise of its constituent power, amend any provision of the Constitution by addition, variation, or repeal. An amendment of the Constitution can only be carried out through a Bill introduced for that purpose in either House of Parliament. Such a Bill must be passed by a majority of the total membership of each House, and by a majority of not less that two-thirds of the members of each House present and voting. It is then presented to the President who shall give his assent and thereupon the Constitution stands amended in accordance with the terms of the Bill.

The following provisions of the Constitution may be amended only if the amendment is also ratified by atleast half of the State Legislatures before the amendment bill is presented for the President's assent -

(a) Election of the President,

(b) Executive Power of the Union and of States,

(c) Union Judiciary, High Courts for States and UTs,

(d) Legislative Relations between Union and States,

(e) Any List in the Seventh Schedule,

(f) Representation of States in Parliament,

(g) Provisions of Amendment of the Constitution.

31.1. Basic Structure Doctrine

The power of Parliament to amend the Constitution is not unlimited or unfetter. This power to amend is provided by the Constitution itself. Hence it cannot be exercised to abrogate or destroy the fundamentals features or the Basic structure of the Constitution.

Though all the provisions of the Constitution including the Fundamental Rights can be amended, there are features or framework of the Constitution which is beyond the amending power of Parliament.

The Basic Structure doctrine has been interpreted over time to include following features of the Constitution as part of the basic structure

(a) Judicial review

(b) Democracy

(c) Free and fair elections based on adult franchise

(d) The rule of law

(e) Harmony and balance between fundamental rights and directive principles

(f) Judicial Independence

(g) Equality

It is pertinent to note that it is not an amendment of a particular article, but rather, an amendment that adversely affects or destroys the wider principles of the Constitution, such as democracy, secularism, equality, or republicanism, or the one that changes the identity of the Constitution that is impermissible under this doctrine.

LAW OF TORTS

1. Introduction

The word "Tort" is derived from Latin word "Tortum" meaning "Wrong". It's meaning, for legal purpose, is a legal wrong or injury.

1.1. Need for Law of Torts

Law of torts creates a balance between individual's freedom of action and society's interest of security. The law provides for freedom to the extent it does not damage social order or causes injury to the people around.

The law of torts does so by providing for pecuniary compensation for injuries to person and property. The compensation is recoverable by the process of law. This compensation shifts the loss from the 'victim' to the person who caused it.

Tort differs from crime as it is redressed by compensation or damages, while crimes are punished by way of imprisonment or fine or other means. At times, the same wrong may be a tort as well as a crime concurrently, for which both actions may be initiated.

Tort also differs from breach of contract. The law of contract deals with rights and duties arising out of agreement of parties. While, law of torts deal with rights created by operation of law and duties imposed on persons in general.

2. DEFINITION

Salmond has defined Tort as a civil wrong for which remedy is common law action for unliquidated damages and which is not exclusively breach of Contract, breach of Trust or other mere equitable obligations.

Although the above definition may appear technical, but the main ingredients of tort are -

2.1. Civil Wrong

Tort is a civil wrong in the sense it is different from criminal wrong or Crime, for which Criminal prosecution may be launched and the chief idea is to punish the wrong doer by way of imprisonment or fine. In civil wrong, there is sanction in form of damages or compensation, restitution, injunction etc.

Civil Wrong presupposes Legal Right. Without Right, there can be no wrong. This wrong can be seen as infringement of Right or breach of legal duty. An action for tort may be brought by any person who's right has been infringed or in whose favour the duty existed has been breached.

In this reference following two maxims must be considered -

i. Injuria sine damno i.e. injury without damage

Injury means legal wrong, whereas damage means loss. This maxim speaks of cases where a person's legal right has been infringed although no loss has occurred to him. For example, In a case where a person was the denied his right to vote but the candidate he intended to vote won the election nonetheless, it was held that although there was no loss but the plaintiff was legally wronged and as such could bring an action in tort

ii. Damnum sine injuria i.e. damage without injury

This maxim speaks of cases where a person has incurred loss, but none of his right has been infringed. For example, where a person started a new school in proximity of old one, the old school loses many students and thus suffer damage and monetary loss. But the old school cannot maintain action in tort because there is no legal wrong. No legal right has been infringed nor any duty breached.

2.2. Unliquidated Damages

Damages refer to measure of harm. Since, under tort law, the the measure of injury cannot be predefined, hence the damages are in this very nature unliquidated i.e. not pre-ascertained. Here, a reference may be made to contractual liability where parties may make a genuine pre-estimate of loss in case of its breach. But in tort, the damages are determinable only after the incident actually occurs.

3. GENERAL ELEMENTS IN TORT

There are two basic elements in Tort, Namely Act or Physical Element and Mental Element.

3.1. Physical Element

Act refers to movement of body, living or dead, or a part of it, but not merely a thought, intention or a dream. Act, in common parlance, denotes activity or action. But legally, Act can be both positive as well as negative. That is, in law, Act includes omission. One may say that even when one chooses not to act, he infact acts the other way round or the act is one of rest or lethargy. Acts and omissions may be understood as events under Human control as against Natural events such as rising of the Sun, Earthquake etc.

Any act cannot amount to tort unless it is done or in negative sense, where it was a duty, the same is omitted. A mere thought or intention or ill-will towards someone without any action in furtherance of it cannot amount to Civil Wrong. Though mere sharing of such idea or thought, in certain cases, may be sufficient to be held liable. In such cases, the sharing is sufficient act.

It is worth noting that although act includes omission but the law generally does not impose liability for omission. But where the law lays down a duty of action, its omission is accountable under the law.

Take, for example, a person "A" is drowning in a Pool. A person "B: standing nearby and watching the incident and despite having the ability to save the first person, omits to do so. B incurs no liability unless he was appointed as a Life-guard, in which case it would have been his duty to try and save the person from drowning.

Further, an act may be voluntary or involuntary. Voluntary means originating out of volition i.e. something one chooses to do or not do, over which the person has control although all its results may not be foreseen.

Involuntary acts are those where the actor lacks the power to control his actions and involuntary omissions are those where the actor's lack of power to control his actions renders him unable to do the act required. An Involuntary act does not give rise to any liability.

3.2. Mental Element

To bring an action under Tort, the act must be voluntary coupled with a mental element such as Malice, Intention, Negligence or Motive. The only exceptions are Strict and Absolute Liability, to which we shall come to at a later stage. First, we shall see different mental elements.

Malice

Malice means ill-will. In law, it is used in two different senses. Firstly, Intentional wrong or Malice in Law. It refers to an act done wrongfully, and without reasonable and probable censure, and not, as in common parlance, an act dictated by angry feeling or vindictive motive. It is in its nature implied i.e. law infers it from circumstances. Secondly, Malice may refer to improper motive or Malice in Fact.

Intention

Intention is an internal fact. It is what goes in the mind of the doer and no direct evidence of the same is available. In an intentional act, the doer has both the knowledge and desire of the consequences.

Negligence

An act is negligent when the consequences are not adverted to though a reasonable person would have foreseen them. For example, Driving a car fast on a busy lane. Though the driver may not intend causing harm to anyone, but a reasonable person can foresee such a catastrophe.

Recklessness or Gross Negligence

When the consequences are adverted to though not desired and there is indifference towards them or willingness to run the risk, it amounts to recklessness. It is often equated with Intention because the negligence is so gross, it is deemed that the person intended the very act or consequence.

Motive

Motive is the ulterior object or purpose of doing an act. It differs from Intention which is immediate. It is the motive that gives rise to Intention and not the other way round. Motive is concrete Intention is abstract. Motive is driving force behind all actions.

Generally, Motive is irrelevant. A person may cause injury to another despite having best of motives. Also, an an action may be perfectly legal despite bad motive. The law has greater regard for the act itself rather than its motive.

Illustration:

If a man throws a stone at a woman, his trespass to her person is intentional; that he threw it because she had jilted him would be motive and immaterial as such. If he did not throw the stone for purpose of hitting her but ought to have foreseen that it was likely that the stone could hit her, his act would be unintentional but nevertheless negligent. If the stone hit her solely because it rebounded off a tree at which it he had thrown it his conduct would be voluntary and hit accidental. But if, while he was holding the stone in his hand, a third party seized his arm and by twisting it compelled him to release his hold on it, whereupon it fell on the woman, his conduct would be involuntary and could not give rise to liability on his part.

4. CLASSIFICATION OF TORTS

All torts can be classified into three broad categories:

4.1. Malfeasance

These are unlawful acts and are actionable per se, that is, without proof of negligence.

4.2. Misfeasance

Misfeasance is improper way of doing the act which cause damage. This happens when one's action is the result of negligence.

4.3. Non-feasance

Non-feasance is wrong of omission. A suit does not lie for them unless the law imposes a duty to act.

5. GENERAL EXCEPTIONS

(JUSTIFICATION OF TORTS)

We have understood, what tort is and what are its elements. Now, we come to its general exceptions. These are the grounds on which a person committing a wrongful act is absolved from his liability to make good or compensate for the loss caused to the other. These are important because when one complains of a wrongful act, the other may deny the commission of the act or plead that his case his covered under exceptions and thus cannot be held liable. They are as follows -

5.1. Leave & License – Volenti non fit injuria

Legally nothing is an injury to which a person consents. In other words, where the sufferer is willing, no injury is done. A man cannot complain of harm to the chances of which he has exposed himself with knowledge and of his free will. The application of the maxim is not dependent upon any valid contract but upon the competence of the decision making capacity of the person at the time the consent was given.

A simple illustration of this defence is the consent that a sportsperson impliedly gives to sustain an injury during the game play so long it is played fairly. So, a cricket fielder sustaining injury while trying to catch the ball is the result of the risk he understood right at the onset of the game. And, as a result, the batman hitting the ball is not liable for the same.

But where, in a football game, a player's foul play injures another and causes injury such as fracture, the first player will be liable for tort, as the consent of the injured player was limited to fair play and not extend to foul play or reckless disregard of player's safety.

It is worth noting that this consent need not be taken down in writing, it which case it would be contractual. But the consent is implied from the actions of the person. Now, to understand the extent of consent, one need not go into the nitty-gritty of the law. But the test of common knowledge and experience is sufficient. So where, a person challenged an old man to fight and gave a severe blow to his eye, it cannot be said that the old man had given consent to such an injury.

Similarly, if there is a statutory duty (duty laid down by statute or legislation), the above maxim will have no application in case of breach of the same.

Also, the maxim does not apply where plaintiff has under an exigency caused by defendant's wrongful misconduct, consciously and deliberately faced a risk, even of death, to rescue another from imminent danger of personal injury or death, whether the person endangered is one to whom he owes a duty of protection, as a member of his family, or is a mere stranger to whom he owes no such specific duty. The rescuer will not be deprived of his remedy merely because the risk which he runs is not the same as that run by the person whom he rescues. But where there is no need to take any risk, the person suffering the harm cannot recover damages.

5.2. Necessity

Necessity knows no law. An act which must necessarily be done does not entail liability.

A necessity can be Public Necessity which is based on maxim – salus populi suprema lex, that is welfare of the people is the supreme law. Examples of public necessity are pulling down of houses or cutting down of trees to prevent spreading of fire, Goods thrown overboard to save the ship or its passengers.

It is only in cases of existing, immediate and over-whelming public necessity that any such right exists. This defence is not available to a defendant whose negligence has created or contributed to the necessity.

Private necessity may also give rise to a defence of necessity.

Third group of cases are concerned with action taken as a matter of necessity to assist another person without his consent. Say, for example, A is walking on the road, when a car is about to hit him. B, seeing this, drags A towards side and rescues him from the car collision, but in doing so tears A's shirt. Now, although B's action has damaged A's shirt but B is not liable to compensate A for the shirt, as his action was necessitated by the on-coming car. Similarly, medical treatment of an unconscious person even without his consent gives rise to no liability as same is under compelling circumstances.

5.3. Inevitable Accident

An "Inevitable Accident" or "unavoidable accident" is that which could not possibly be prevented by the exercise of ordinary care, caution and skill. It is based on rule of prudence that a person must guard against reasonable probabilities but they are not bound to guard against remote or fantastic possibilities. The term "accident" presupposes their origin in whole or part in human agency.

To understand, one can take a simple illustration. Say, two dogs belonging to two individuals are engaged in fighting when one of them uses a stick to separate them and accidentally hits the other individual causing him severe injury. The first individual, since could not have foreseen such a casualty, cannot be held liable towards the second.

Similarly, when a person A fires a bullet which hits a series of object and then ultimately injures a person B standing altogether in a different location, A may not be held liable. But it will be a question of fact whether A employed necessary care and caution which the situation demanded. So, if you shoot an arrow on the apple placed on someone's head, be ready to be held accountable, as the running the risk amounts to recklessness and is well foreseen.

5.4. Act of God or vis major

Act of God is similar to inevitable accidents the only difference id that the act of God are those that are occasioned by the elementary forces of Nature unconnected with the agency of man.

Act of God is defined as such a direct violent, sudden and irresistible act of nature as could not, by any amount of ability, have been foreseen, or if foreseen, could not by any amount of Human care and skill have been resisted. For example, earthquake, storm, lightening, extraordinary rainfall, extraordinary high tide.

It is necessary that the phenomenon should be extraordinary. So if, a roof brick falls on a passerby's head in ordinary rains of the region, this defence will not be available to the occupier of the house who has neglected his duty to keep up such repairs. Similarly, when a hotel room on a beach resort is flooded with water in ordinary tide, this defence is unavailable to the Hotel owner as the risk is foreseeable and the cause of damage is ordinary.

It is worth noting that it is not necessary that the natural phenomenon should be unique or occur for the first time. But it must be extraordinary regard being held to the general climatic and natural conditions of the place.

5.5. Plaintiff himself a wrong doer

Where the person seeking remedy under tort is himself the wrong doer, the defendant (person against whom legal action has been initiated) may put plaintiff's wrong doing as defence. For example, A is driving his car negligently and thereby hits B who was carrying a briefcase. In the collision, B is startled and drops his case which breaks A's car's headlight. Now, since A is himself at fault, he cannot claim compensation from B for the said broken light.

This defence may be a total defence or a proportionate reduction in damages depending upon the facts of the case. But it must be understood that the plaintiff is not denied compensation unless some unlawful act or conduct on his own part is connected with the harm suffered by him as a part of the same transaction.

Take, for example, A trespasses B's house by climbing his wall. In doing so, A's trousers get torned. B will not be held liable for A' trousers. But if B has placed spring guns in his gardens without notice, and the same fires injuring A, B will be held liable for the said injury. Nonetheless, B may also sue A for trespass.

5.6. Act of State

We already know that Law presupposes State and State is the machinery for Justice, that the law originates from the State's desire and standard of Justice. Nonetheless, an act of State by itself cannot result in Injury.

Though with growth of Human Rights, the idea of State has undergone a lot of change and even the State does not have unlimited authority over its citizens. Particularly, in modern constitutional democracies, Constitutional Law sets out certain limitations over State's authority. There is an arena of civil liberties that cannot be encroached upon by the State or its agencies. These are, what is referred to in Indian Constitution as, Fundamental Rights. These are basic rights necessary for human development and cannot be alienated or parted with.

But despite fundamental rights, there is a plethora of region where individual rights must give way to the state action derived from larger interest of the society. So, if in a riot, a Police Officer uses firearm well within his authority and somehow ends up injuring an innocent or his chattels, the State will come in to protect his wrong doing. Similarly, a Judge presiding over in a judicial proceedings cannot commit any wrong. Their actions are protected under law by way of immunity.

It is worth noting that presently State engages in a variety of activities which are essentially business. And the State or its corporations engaged in such business activities cannot claim this defence because while acting as such, they are acting similar to an ordinary citizen. It is only for the sovereign acts of state (such as Law and order, Justice administration, War) that this defence can be used.

5.7. Private Defence

Every person has a right to defend his own person, property, or possession against an unlawful harm. This may even be done for a wife or husband, or parent or child, a master or servant, and even for strangers in need out of empathy. But the act must be one of defence and not an offence in itself. The means adopted to protect oneself or one's property must be reasonable i.e. proportionate to the threat and that the danger must be real and imminent.

5.8. Trifle Act or act causing slight harm

This defence is based on maxim 'de minimis non curat lex', that is, law does not take in account of trifles. Nothing is a wrong which a person of ordinary sense and temper would not complain. This has no application where there is injury to a legal right.

6. SOME COMMON TORTS

Law recognizes many torts and assign specific names to them. These torts have specific ingredients and may have special defences apart from general defences discussed earlier. It must be understood that wherever the recognizes a Civil right and protects the same from infringement by people at large, an action under tort may be initiated; although no specific name has yet been assigned to the said wrongful act or tort. Conversely, whenever law prescribes a duty towards persons generally, the breach of the same is redressable by action for tort. This is because there exists a general law of tort apart from law of torts.

In other words, law is capable of creating new torts and such a creation is possible by the hands of Judges themselves, and no Statute need be enacted for the same. This is another distinction between tort and crime, where an act is punishable only when it falls within the four walls of a specific offence. That is, there does not exist any general law of crime prescribing punishment for acts, howsoever wrongful or outrageous they may appear, unless there is an existing statute prescribing the same.

Now, we shall discuss about some common torts.

7. TRESPASS TO PERSON

Trespass to person is intentional causing of Injury to person or body of individual. Thus its essentials are -

(i) Intentional act

(ii) Causing of Injury

(iii) To person or body of individual

For example, where a woman is hit and her leg broken by a car driven negligently, the tort of trespass to person is not made out as the injury is not intentional. However, the driver may be liable for negligence (another tort). Most common form of trespass to person are – Assault, Battery and False Imprisonment.

7.1. Assault

An assault is an attempt or threat to do a corporeal hurt to another, coupled with an apparent present ability and intention to do the act. Thus its essentials are -

(a) Intentional act

(b) Attempt or threat

(c) Corporeal hurt or bodily injury to another

(d) Apparent present ability to do the act.

Intention as well as the act makes the assault. Thus, a mere tap on the shoulder is no assault. But when A makes a fist and tries to punch B in face, though misses, is liable for assault.

Mere words do not amount to assault. Though they may amount to criminal intimidation (another tort). But words along with gestures may amount to assault. Some common examples of assault are showing of fist with anger, raising a baton with intent to hit, aiming a gun with intent to shoot, unleashing a dog, etc.

7.2. Battery

A battery is the intentional and direct application of any physical force to the person of another. In short, Battery is a successful assault. What is necessary is that the wrongful act must involve physical contact, but no bodily harm is necessary. Even slight touching of another in anger is battery. For example, When A throws a water balloon on B, it is assault. If the Balloon hits B, it is battery although the balloon may not have bursted.

Some common examples of battery are slapping, pushing, throwing something, spitting on face, overturning the carriage in which person is seated, upsetting ladder on which one is standing, whipping the horse one is riding upon, causing another to be medically examined against his will, forcible removal from a place one is legally entitled to stay, etc.

Some examples where the act is not battery can be pushing of another in a crowd if it is not deliberate, accidental touch, etc.

7.3. False imprisonment

False imprisonment is a total restraint of the liberty of a person, for however, short a time, without lawful excuse. Its essentials are -

(a) Total restraint of the liberty,

(b) Without sufficient lawful justification,

(c) Period of detention is immaterial,

(d) The restraint may be either Actual, that is, physical or Constructive, that is by mere show of authority,

(e) Person unlawfully detained need not have knowledge that he was under detention,

(f) False imprisonment is actionable without proof of damage.

If a person gets another arrested by police by making a false complaint, he is liable for false imprisonment. Where a person is arrested by police on information by a person, he is not liable unless he himself was instigator, promoter and active inciter of the arrest, which would make him liable. The reason is that the Intention is an essential ingredient of tort of Trespass to person. Unless, the intention can be gathered from the act, trespass is not made out.

It is also to note that if a person is arrested without warrant and is produced before a Magistrate. Now, if the magistrate grants remand, tort of false imprisonment cannot be made out. After remand, the remedy is action for Malicious prosecution (another tort).

8. DEFAMATION

Man considers his honour and reputation more valuable than even his physical safety. The law on Defamation creates a balance between protection of individual reputation and society's interest in truth and freedom of speech.

A defamatory statement is a statement calculated to expose a person to hatred, contempt or ridicule, or to injure him in his trade, business, profession, calling or office, or to cause him to be shunned or avoided in society. Defamation is of two kinds – Slander and Libel.

A Slander is a false and defamatory statement by spoken words or gestures tending to injure the reputation of another. A libel is a publication of a false and defamatory statement tending to injure reputation of another expressed in some permanent form.

The ingredients of libel are -

(i) False statement

(ii) In writing or some permanent concrete form such as movie, caricature, statue, newspaper etc.

(iii) Defamatory, that is

(a) expose the plaintiff to hatred, contempt, ridicule, or obloquy, or

(b) tend to injure him in his profession or trade, or

(c) cause him to be shunned or avoided by his neighbours.

(iv) Statement must refer to the plaintiff

(v) Publication of such statement, that is, communication of defamatory statement to some third person or persons generally.

8.1 Defences to tort of defamation

A number of defences or justifications are available in a case of defamation. They are as follows -

1. Truth of the statement.

Truth of a statement is a complete defence to defamation. But the statement must be true in all its parts and as a whole. The motive behind making such a statement is irrelevant. But where the statement is false, it is immaterial that the person saying it honestly believed it to be true.

2. Fair and bona fide comment.

A fair and bona fide comment on a matter of public interest is no libel. That is, legitimate criticism is no tort. Examples of matters of public interest are Affairs of the State, Political issues, Religious Institutions, Public conduct of ministers or other officials of government, Administration of Justice, Books, Works of Art, Theatre and public entertainment. But the comment must be a fair one. It must be based on the facts. Take for Example, A says of a book published by Z - "Z's book is foolish; Z must be a weak man. Z's book is indecent; Z must be a man of impure mind." A is within the exception.

But if A says-"I am not surprised that Z's book is foolish and indecent, for he is a weak man and a libertine." A is not within this exception, inasmuch as the opinion which he expresses of Z's character is an opinion not founded on Z's book.

3. Absolute Privilege

Privilege means that a special advantage or immunity or benefit reserved exclusively to a particular person or group. In reference to defamation, Privilege means that the person stands in such a relation to the facts of the case that he is justified in saying or writing it.

A statement is absolutely privileged when no action lies for it even though it is false and defamatory, and made with express malice. Occasions where this absolute privilege may be exercised are -

(a) Parliamentary proceedings

(b) Judicial proceedings

(c) Military and Naval proceedings

(d) Executive proceedings of the State

4. Qualified Privilege

A statement is said to have a qualified privilege when no action lies for it even though it is false and defamatory, unless the plaintiff proves express malice. The following are cases of qualified privilege -

(a) When the circumstances are such that the defendant is under a duty of making a communication to a third person who has a corresponding interest in receiving it.

(b) Where the defendant has an interest to protect and the third person has a duty to protect that interest.

(c) Communication made in cases of confidential relationship such as Husband-wife, Parent-child, Guardian-ward, Master-servant, Advocate-client, etc.

(d) Communication made in self protection or word of caution.

(e) Protection of common interest.

(f) Communication made to persons in public position.

(g) Fair reporting of Parliamentary or Judicial proceedings.

9. FRAUD OR DECEIT

The making of a representation which a party knows to be untrue, and which is intended, or is calculated, to induce another to act on the faith of it, so that he may incur damage, is Fraud in law. Thus deceit is concerned with fraudulent representation. A representation to be fraudulent must be -

(a) Untrue statement,

(b) Defendant knows it to be untrue or is indifferent as to its truth,

(c) Intended or calculated to induce other to act,

(d) Other person acts and suffers damage.

In short, Deceit consists in "leading a man into damage by wilfully or recklessly causing him to believe and act upon falsehood".

Mere non-disclosure of a fact is not fraud. But where there is a duty to disclose, non-disclosure of the same may amount to fraud. The tort of fraud involves a statement of fact and not merely of opinion. There must be active inducement. The representation must be made with knowledge of its falsehood or without belief in its truth. It is also necessary to prove that the plaintiff suffered damage by acting upon untruth. If the defendant honestly believes in the truth of the statement, there cannot be fraud even when the grounds to believe so are insufficient.

10. MALICIOUS PROSECUTION

Malicious prosecution consists in instituting unsuccessful criminal proceedings maliciously and without reasonable or probable cause, which causes actual damage to the party prosecuted, as a natural consequence of the prosecution complained of. The law on Malicious Prosecution creates a balance between freedom that every person should have in bringing criminals to justice and the need for restraining false accusations against innocent persons. The tort is limited to unsuccessful criminal proceedings, and does not apply to malicious civil proceedings.

The essentials of malicious prosecution are -

(a) The Plaintiff was prosecuted.

(b) He was prosecuted by the defendant.

(c) Proceedings terminated in the favour of the plaintiff.

(d) Prosecution was instituted against him without any reasonable or probable cause.

(e) Prosecution was instituted with malicious intention, that is, with wrongful in fact.

(f) Plaintiff suffered damage to his reputation, or safety of person, or security of his property.

10.1. Prosecution

Prosecution, here, does not mean prosecution in legal sense, that is, trial. But the proceedings must reach such a stage at which damage results to the plaintiff. It is enough that a charge is made before a Magistrate with a view to induce him to entertain it.

10.2. By the Defendant

The defendant must have set the Judicial Process in motion and should have been actively instrumental in bringing about the criminal proceedings. If the complainant mere gives information to the police which he believes to be true and does nothing more, he is not liable for malicious prosecution.

Say, for example, there is a theft at A's shop. A gives information to the police of theft and lays suspicion upon B. But does not take active part in the proceedings. A cannot be called the prosecutor.

10.3. Termination in Plaintiff's favour

It is not necessary that the plaintiff was acquitted but the proceedings must terminate in his favour. He may have been discharged, complaint dismissed or the proceedings quashed altogether. But they must not be pending.

10.4. Without reasonable or probable cause.

To understand what is without any reasonable or probable cause, one needs to understand what is reasonable or probable cause. For reasonable or probable cause, there must be -

(a) Honest belief in guilt of accused,

(b) The belief must be based on honest conviction of existence of circumstances,

(c) There must be grounds for a fairly cautious man to believe so,

(d) Circumstances so believed and relied upon must be reasonable for belief in the guilt of accused.

That is to say, if a person takes care to have adequate information of facts, honestly believes in the truth of his allegation, and facts are such that a prima facie case is made out, it would certainly be inferred that his conduct is reasonable.

If the charge is false, it is upon the defendant to show that he had reasonable and sufficient cause for making the accusation.

10.5. Malice

Malice means spite or ill-will towards a person or improper motive. It can also be any improper purpose which motivates the prosecutor, such as malign before the public. It is a wish to injure the party rather than to vindicate the law.

Malice may be inferred from absence of honest belief of guilt and want of reasonable and probable cause for prosecution.

10.6. Damage

"Damage" is not confined to monetary loss. Damage may be to -

(a) Person's reputation,

(b) Person's life, limb or liberty,

(c) Person's property, for example, expense incurred in defence.

11. TRESPASS TO LAND

Dictionary meaning of trespass is to enter unlawfully on someone's property. Trespass is wrongful interference with land which is in the possession of the plaintiff. To constitute a wrong of trespass neither force, nor unlawful intention, nor actual damage, nor breaking of an enclosure is necessary. Every invasion of private property, be it ever so minute, is a Trespass

Trespass may be committed in any of the following three forms -

(a) By entering upon the land of the plaintiff or

(b) By remaining on such land, or

(c) By doing any other act affecting sole possession of the plaintiff. Such as -

(i) Placing any object on it or

(ii) Throwing any object on it or

(iii) Constructing a projection in air space over the land of another, or

(iv) Doing anything on it without lawful justification.

Trespass is a wrong against possession, and in certain cases even the owner may be held liable for the damage to the person in possession of the immovable property.

11.1. Remedies to Trespass

The law provides for certain remedies to a person whose property has been subject matter of the wrong of trespass. He may -

(a) Bring an action for trespass against the wrong-doer,

(b) Forcibly defend his possession against the trespasser,

(c) Forcibly eject him.

11.2. Defences to Tort of Trespass

The law recognises certain acts as exception to trespass. That is, when an entry is made on property of another under certain circumstances, they do not amount to tort of trespass. They are as follows -

1. Licence (i.e. Permission)

2. Authority of Law

3. Act of necessity

4. Self-defence

5. Re-entry on land

6. Re-taking of goods and chattels

7. Abating a nuisance

13. NUISANCE

Nuisance means anything done to the hurt or annoyance of the lands, tenements or hereditaments of another, and not amount to trespass.

According to Winfield, Nuisance is an unlawful interference with one's use or enjoyment of land or of some right over or in connection with it. Examples of nuisance are disturbing noise, bad smelling fumes, polluting water, overhanging trees, vibrations, sparks, etc.

Nuisance basically is an interference with the comfort of occupiers of land but every interference is not actionable nuisance if the conduct of the defendant is not unreasonable. Some minor discomforts which are parts of the social life in crowded cities, have to be endured, and looking to circumstances of time, place and persons they may not be regarded as nuisance by courts. Whether there is in fact nuisance or not has to be judged from the point of view of time, place, and other circumstances.

Nuisance is of two kinds: Public Nuisance and Private Nuisance.

13.1. Public Nuisance

Public or common nuisance is an act or omission, which causes any common injury, danger, or annoyance to the public or to the people in general who dwell or occupy property in the vicinity, or which must necessarily cause injury, obstruction, danger or annoyance to persons who may have occasion to use any public right. From the above definition, ingredients of public nuisance are -

(a) act or omission,

(b) causes injury, danger, or annoyance,

(d) to the public or to the people.

Public nuisance is a criminal act. An individual may sue for public nuisance only if he has suffered some damage that is particular, direct and substantial. In case of no special damage, two or more persons with the permission of the court may bring a civil action for tort.

13.2. Private Nuisance

Private nuisance is the using or authorising the use of one's property or of any thing under one's control, so as to injuriously affect an owner or occupier of property by physically injuring his property or affecting its enjoyment by interfering materially with his health, comfort and convenience.

It is important to note that a right to commit private nuisance may be acquired by prescription (long use) as an easement.

13.3. Remedies

The law provides for following remedies against private nuisance -

(a) Damages or compensation

(b) Injunction

(c) Extra-judicial remedy of abatement of nuisance by himself.

14. NEGLIGENCE

The tort of negligence is different from the Mental element, negligence, discussed before. Negligence, as a tort, is the breach of a duty caused by the omission to do something which a reasonable man, guided by those considerations which ordinarily regulate the conduct of human affairs would do, or doing something which a prudent and reasonable man would not do.

According to Winfield, Negligence as a tort is the breach of a legal duty to take care which results in damage, undesired by the defendant to the plaintiff. From the definition, one can gather following ingredients of the tort of negligence -

(i) A legal duty,

(ii) Duty to exercise due care,

(iii) Duty on the party complained of,

(iv) Duty towards the party complaining,

(v) Breach of said duty, and

(vi) Consequential damage

The law takes no cognizance of carelessness in the abstract. It concerns itself with carelessness only where there is a duty to take care and where failure in that duty has caused damage. In such circumstances carelessness assumes the legal quality of negligence and entails the consequences in law.

One must take reasonable care to avoid acts or omissions which you can reasonably foresee would be likely to injure your neighbour. Neighbour is not limited to persons dwelling in one's locality. It is one who is affected by the negligent act. He is one who must be in contemplation when the mind is directed to the negligent act. So, while you are driving a car, all persons in proximity and may be hit by your car are your neighbours for this purpose. And you must exercise care for all of these persons.

Damage caused by negligent act must not be remote but a direct one. The test is one of foreseeablilty and standard of care is that of a reasonable and prudent man. Thus, every act must be performed with care that a reasonable and prudent man would employ in those circumstances and guard against foreseeable dangers or consequences.

LAW OF CONTRACT

1. Introduction

The term 'Contract' is of common parlance meaning 'to make bargain'. In law, it has a specific definition – An agreement enforceable by law is a Contract.

Agreement again means, in common parlance, as something agreed upon. In law, every promise and every set of promises forming consideration of each other is an agreement. This definition employs two terms – Promise and Consideration.

Promise is an accepted proposal. Proposal means to make an offer. Legally speaking, when one person signifies to another his willingness to do or to abstain from doing something with a view to obtain the assent of that other, he is said to make a proposal. Acceptance means signifying assent or agreeing to the proposal brought forth.

Consideration is price of the promise. It is in nature of quid pro quo, that is, something for something. It is the price for which the promise of other is brought and what make the promise enforceable. In law, When at the desire of the promisor (person making the proposal), the promisee (person accepting the proposal) or any other person has done or abstained from doing, or does or abstains from doing, or promises to do or to abstain from doing, something, such act or abstinence or promise is called a Consideration for the promise.

Thus, we mathematically represent these relations as -

Promise = Proposal + Acceptance

Agreement = Promise + Consideration

Contract = Agreement + Legal Enforceability

As far as enforceability of an agreement is concerned, all agreements are contracts if they are made by the free consent of parties competent to contract, for a lawful consideration and with a lawful object, and are not hereby expressly declared to be void. Thus, Legal Enforceability of Agreement requires following prerequisites -

(a) Intention to Contract,

(b) Competent Parties,

(c) Free Consent,

(d) Lawful Object,

(e) Lawful Consideration, and

(f) Not expressly declared void

Now, we shall take up each of the these elements of Agreement and Enforceability individually.

2. PROPOSAL

The word 'proposal' or 'offer' means to give option to someone to agree or deny. In terms of Contracts, a person is said to make a proposal when he signifies to another his willingness to do or abstain from doing anything with a view to obtaining the assent of that other to such act or abstinence. From this definition, one can make out following ingredients of a Proposal -

(a) It is an expressions of willingness,

(b) To do or to abstain from doing an act, that is, it may be for doing an act or making an omission, and

(c) Expressed with a view to obtain the assent of the other party to whom the offer is made.

For example -

(i) "A" offers to sell his car to "B". This is proposal as it conveys A's willingness to do an act and also solicits B's assent.

(ii) "A" offers to "B" to omit bidding at an auction event, where B intends to bid, for payment of a sum. This is proposal.

(iii) Where "A" says to "B" that he intends to marry B by the end of the year. This is no offer, unless, he also asks "Will you marry me?"

2.1. Classification of Proposal/Offer

Offer can be classified as general offer, specific offer, cross offer, counter offer, standing/open/continuing offer.

(a) General offer

It is an offer made to public at large. Until the general offer is retracted or withdrawn, it can be accepted by anyone. Thus, it is continuing is nature. For example, SMS Code to win contests are general offers. Any person who sends the code inside the packet is actually accepting the general offer. Similarly, where A advertises that he will Rs 500/- to anyone who brings back his lost dog. He makes a general offer. A vending machine at the airport, A bus at the bus stop ready to ply are in their nature general offers.

(b) Special/Specific offer

Where an offer is made to a particular person, it is a specific offer. Only that person can accept such specific offer, as it is exclusive to him.

(c) Cross offer

Cross offers are offers made to each other in ignorance of offer of the other. For example, if A makes a proposal to B to sell his car at a specified price and B, without knowing proposal of A, makes a proposal to purchase the same car at the same price. The offers are cross offers. And one is not acceptance of other. Nor is there any binding contract between them by mere exchange of proposals.

(d) Counter offer

Counter offer is an offer made in response to another offer. If, upon receipt of an offer, the offeree instead of accepting it straightway, imposes conditions which have the effect of modifying or varying the offer, he is said to have made a counter offer.

For example, A says to B – "Will you buy my car for Rs. 50,000/-?" And B replies - "I will do it for Rs. 45,000/-." B is making a counter offer. Counter offers amounts to rejection of the original offer. Thus, B cannot, at a later stage, say that he accepts A's offer for Rs. 50,000/- and bind him with his proposal.

(e) Standing or continuing or open offer

An offer which is kept open for acceptance for a certain period of time is known as standing or continuing or open offer. For example, A offers to supply coal to B for running thermal power plant for a period of one year at a particular price. This is a continuing offer. And each time an order is placed, the same is acceptance.

2.2. Essentials of a Valid Proposal/Offer

An offer must adhere to certain rules to be a valid offer. They are as follows -

(a) The 'offer' must be with intent to create a legal relationship and not mere social relationship. Thus, an invitation for dinner is not an offer.

(b) The offer must be certain and definite. It must not be vague. For example, where 'A' offers to sell 100 litres of oil, without indicating what kind of oil would be sold, it is a vague offer and hence cannot create any contractual relationship. If however there is a mechanism to end the vagueness, the offer can be treated as valid. Thus, if in the above example if 'A' does not deal in any oil but only in Mustard oil and this is matter of common knowledge, the offer is not vague but a valid offer.

(c) It may be express or implied.

(d) It must be distinguished from an invitation to offer.

(e) The offer must be communicated to the person to whom it is made. This communication may be made by act or omission by which the person intends to communicate, or which has the effect of communicating it. An un-communicated offer cannot be accepted. So, if A writes a letter offering to sell his house for a price to B and keeps the letter in his desk drawer. A does not make an offer since he has not posted the letter.

(f) The offer must be made with a view to obtain the assent of the promisee.

(f) An offer may be conditional. But burden to refute cannot be placed on the promisee. That is, the promisor cannot say that if non-acceptance is not communicated by a certain time the offer would be treated as accepted.

2.3. Invitation to Offer

An offer must be distinguished from a mere invitation to offer. An offer is definite and expresses willingness with a view to obtain assent and if assent is given thereto, the contract is concluded.

An invitation to offer is an act precedent to making an offer. An invitation to offer is - "...an expression of willingness to negotiate. A person making an invitation to treat does not intend to be bound as soon as it is accepted by the person to whom the statement is addressed."

An invitation to offer gives rise to an offer after due negotiation and it cannot be per se accepted. In an invitation to offer there is no expression of willingness by the offeror to be bound by his offer. It is only a proposal of certain terms on which he is willing to negotiate. It is not capable of being accepted as it is.

The essence of an invitation to offer is that the offer is actually made by the seller. For example, An advertisement in newspaper. The reason is that it does not make business sense for advertisements to be offers, as the person making the advertisement may find himself in a situation where he would be contractually obliged to sell more goods than he actually owned.

Similarly, a display of clothes in a shop, of goods in an auction, and even advertisements screaming "Offer! 50% Off on All Shirts!" is actually an invitation to treat, and not an offer.

Therefore, an invitation to offer 'evolves' into a contract in a different manner than an offer. Initially, it is an invitation to offer, say by a display of goods and their prices. When a person makes an offer that is good enough and the seller 'accepts' it, it becomes a contract.

The test to decide whether a statement is an 'offer' or 'invitation to offer' is to see the 'intention'. If a person who makes the statement has the intention to be bound by it as soon as the other accepts, he is making an offer. If he however intends to do some other act, he is making only an invitation to offer.

Where the owner of the property had said that he would not accept less than Rs. 6000/- for it. The statement does not indicate any offer but only an invitation to offer. Similarly, in an auction, goods put up for auction are invitation while the bids are offer. Some key examples of Invitation to offer are -

(i) Menu card of a restaurant showing the prices of food items.

(ii) Railway Chart setting out train timings and fares.

(iii) Government Tender.

(iv) An invitation by a company to the public to subscribe for its shares.

(v) Recruitment advertisement inviting application.

(vi) Quotation of prices sent in reply to a query regarding price.

3. ACCEPTANCE

A proposal or offer is said to have been accepted when the person to whom the proposal is made signifies his assent to the said proposal. Act of acceptance lies in signifying one's assent to the proposal.

According to Sir William Anson "Acceptance is to offer what a lighted match is to a train of gun powder". That is what acceptance triggers cannot be recalled or undone. But there is a choice to the person who had the train to remove it before the match is applied. It in effect means that the offer can be withdrawn just before it is accepted. Acceptance converts the offer into a promise and then it is too late to revoke it. The significance of this is an offer by itself cannot create any legal relationship but it is the acceptance by the offeree which creates a legal relationship.

3.1. Essentials of a Valid Acceptance

(a) For a valid acceptance, there must be knowledge of offer. Without knowledge of offer, there can be no acceptance. For example, where a person finds a missing dog without knowledge of award, he cannot claim the award afterwards.

(b) The acceptance must be communicated. To conclude a contract between the parties, the acceptance must be communicated in some perceptible form.

(c) Acceptance must be made by the promisee himself or any person having authority to accept on his behalf.

(d) The acceptance must relate specifically to the offer made.

(e) Acceptance must be absolute and unqualified.

(f) It should be expressed in some usual and reasonable manner unless the proposal prescribes the manner in which it must be accepted. If the proposal prescribes the manner in which it must be accepted, then it must be accepted accordingly.

(g) The acceptance must be given within a reasonable time and before the offer lapses.

(h) Acceptance may be express or implied. It may also be expressed by conduct.

(i) But mere silence is not acceptance. As already stated, the burden to refute the offer cannot be placed on the promisee.

Illustrations

(i) A offers to B to sell A's car for Rs. 2 lacs. If B replies - "I shall purchase your car for the said price, if A buys B's motorcycle for Rs. 50000/-." This is no acceptance as it is conditional. By its very nature, it is a counter offer to A, who may accept or deny it.

(ii) If, in the above example, B agrees to purchase the car from A as per his offer if A has a valid Registration Certificate. The acceptance is a valid one. This is because expecting a valid title for the car is not a condition.

(iii) A offers to sell his house to B for Rs 5,00,00/-. B replied purporting to accept the offer but enclosed a cheque for Rs 2,00,000/- only and promises to pay the balance in monthly installments. Acceptance is invalid not being an unqualified one.

(iv) A offers to sell his car to B for Rs. 1,00,000/-. B replied that, "I can pay Rs. 80,000 for it." A's offer stands rejected. Later on, if B decides to pay Rs. 1,00000/-, the same will be a counter offer only as A's offer was already rejected.

(v) A, a trader, receives an order from B. The order is executed accordingly by the trader. A has made acceptance to the offer by his conduct.

(vi) A boards a bus to Delhi. A's conduct amounts to acceptance.

4. COMMUNICATION

Communication is an indispensable element in concluding a contract. There must be effective communication of both 'offer' and 'acceptance' to give rise to a valid contract.

Importance of communication lies in the fact that parties are separated by distance and they employ modes such as post, telegram, fax, email, telephone etc. Effective and proper communication prevents avoidable misunderstanding between parties.

Law gives a lot of importance to "time" element in deciding when the offer and acceptance is complete, and upto what time offer or acceptance may be revoked.

4.1. Communication of offer

Communication of offer is complete when it comes to the knowledge of the person to whom it is made. Knowledge of the offer would materialize when the offer is given in writing or made by word of mouth or by some other conduct. For Example, 'A' writes a letter making a proposal to 'B' to sell his house for Rs. 5 lakhs. The letter is posted on 15th Jan and reaches B on 18th Jan, the offer is said to have been communicated on 18th Jan when B received the letter.

In telephonic communications, communication of offer is complete as soon as the voice is heard by the person receiving the offer.

4.2. Communication of acceptance

Communication of acceptance may be oral or written, that is by way of letters, telegrams, faxes, emails, telephonic conversion. Communication of acceptance can also be done by conduct. For instance, delivery of goods at a price by a seller to a buyer on receipt of tender. The delivery of goods is communication of acceptance by conduct. Similarly, boarding a bus or dropping currency in a vending machine is acceptance by conduct.

But a mere mental unilateral assent in one's own mind would not amount to acceptance. For example, A receives an offer to buy B's house for certain price. A decides to buy the same but does not say anything to B. There is no acceptance as there is no communication of the same.

As to when the communication is complete, the law is that the communication of acceptance is complete -

(a) As against the proposer, when it is put in course of transmission to him so as to be out of the power of the acceptor to withdraw the same;

(b) As against the acceptor, when it comes to the knowledge of the proposer.

The above rule may appear complicated, but can be understood by simple illustration. If in above example where offer is sent by letter, B writes letter of acceptance and posts it on 20th Jan which is received by A on 24th Jan. The communication of acceptance is complete as against A (proposer) on 20$^{th\ Jan}$ and against B (acceptor) on 24th Jan.

Here, A the proposer will be bound by B's acceptance, even if the letter of acceptance is delayed in post or lost in transit. The golden rule is proposer becomes bound by the contract, the moment acceptor has posted the letter of acceptance. But it is necessary that the letter is correctly addressed, sufficiently stamped and duly posted. In such an event the loss of letter in transit, wrong delivery, non delivery etc., will not affect the validity of the contract.

However from the view point of acceptor, he will be bound by his acceptance only when the letter of acceptance has reached the proposer. If there is no delivery of the letter, the acceptance could be treated as having been completed from the viewpoint of proposer but not from the viewpoint of acceptor. This will, however, give rise to an awkward situation where only one party to the contract being treated as bound by the contract though no one would be sure as to where the letter of acceptance had gone.

5. REVOCATION OF OFFER AND ACCEPTANCE

Similar to rules for communication of offer and acceptance, there are rules for communication of revocation of such offer and acceptance.

As far as revocation of proposal is concerned, a proposal may be revoked by -

(a) Communication of notice of revocation.

(b) Lapse of the time prescribed in such proposal or if no time is so prescribed, by the lapse of a reasonable time.

(c) Failure of the acceptor to fulfil a condition precedent to acceptance. For example, A proposes to sell his car to B for Rs. 2 lakhs provided B sells his motorbike A. If B refuses to sell his bike, the offer of A is revoked automatically.

(d) Death or insanity of the proposer, if the fact of his death or insanity comes to the knowledge of the acceptor before acceptance.

A proposal can be revoked at any time before the communication of its acceptance is complete as against the proposer. An acceptance may be revoked at any time before the communication of acceptance is complete as against the acceptor.

This may appear technical. But can be understood from aforesaid example of communications by letter. A may revoke his proposal to B, before B post his letter of acceptance, that is, by 20th Jan and not thereafter. Further, B may revoke his acceptance before the letter of acceptance is received by A, that is, by 24th Jan and not thereafter.

As to time, the communication of revocation (of the proposal or its acceptance) is complete -

(a) as against the person who makes it when it is put into a course of transmission to the person to whom it is made so as to be out of the power of the person who makes it, and

(b) as against the person to whom it is made, when it comes to his knowledge.

6. CONSIDERATION

Consideration is price of the promise. It is in nature of quid pro quo, that is, something for something. It is the price for which the promise of other is brought and promise thus given for value is enforceable. Consideration is "some right, interest, profit or benefit accruing to one party or forbearance, detriment, loss, or responsibility given, suffered or undertaken by the other". This refers to the position of both the promisor, and the promisee in an agreement.

In law, When at the desire of the promisor (person making the proposal), the promisee (person accepting the proposal) or any other person has done or abstained from doing, or does or abstains from doing, or promises to do or to abstain from doing, something, such act or abstinence or promise is called a Consideration for the promise.

From the above definition it can be inferred that -

(a) Consideration is doing or not doing something.

(b) Consideration must be at the desire of the promisor.

(c) Consideration may move from one person to any other person.

(d) Consideration may be past, present or future.

(e) Consideration should be real though not adequate.

For example, A promises to sell his house to B for Rs. 5 lakhs. Here, A is the promisor and B is the promisee. B agrees to buy the house for the said price. Here, B will be the promisor and A will be the promisee. That is, A must part with the house and B must part with Rs. 5 lakhs. Thus, Consideration is mutual and has two sides.

It is also possible that there may not be any identifiable benefit towards consideration. For example, A promises to carry B's goods free of charge and B allows A to carry the same. Here B has suffered a detriment or disadvantage while allowing A to carry his goods. This is sufficient consideration.

Above example shows that Consideration has dual aspect. It is not necessarily a gain or advantage to the promisor but it can even be a loss or detriment to the promisee.

Similarly in a contract of guarantee of Loan, where A applies for a loan from Bank B, and if B insists on a guarantee by G. B gives loan to A on G's guarantee. Here, G will be promisor and B promisee. The benefit conferred on A by B at the guarantee of G, is sufficient consideration for G. In other words B has suffered a detriment which is the consideration for the guarantee of G to repay the loan which B has given to A. Detriment to one is benefit to another.

But Consideration is sine qua non for a contract. In the absence of consideration, a gratuitous promise will not result in an agreement. For example, a promise to subscribe to a charitable cause cannot be enforced.

6.1. Essentials of a Consideration

(i) Consideration must move at the desire of the promisor.

(ii) Consideration can flow either from the promisee or any other person. That is, consideration can legitimately move from a third party. For example, A by a deed of gift made over certain property to her daughter D with condition that A's brother B should be paid annuity by D. In furtherance, D executes a document on the same day agreeing to pay the annuity accordingly, but declined to pay after sometime. B sued D. D contends that there was no consideration from B and hence there was no valid contract. Held, that the consideration did flow from B's Sister A to D. Such consideration from third party is sufficient to enforce the D's promise.

(iii) Consideration may be past, present or future. For example where A pays Rs. 5000/- to B requesting him to deliver certain quantity of rice, to which B agrees. The consideration for B is present (or executed) as A has already paid, while for A, consideration is future (or executory) as B is yet to deliver the rice.

Similarly, when A pays a premium of Rs. 5000/- seeking insurance cover for the year, from the insurance company which the company promises in the event of fire, the consideration paid by A to the insurance company is executed but the promise of insurance company is executory or yet to be executed.

(iv) Consideration may also be constituted in the past acts of promisee, but the act must have been non-gratuitous and also at the desire of the promisor.

(v) Consideration must be real and not illusionary. It must be something of value.

(vi) Consideration need not be adequate. That is to say, consideration need not necessarily be of the same value as of the promise for which it is exchanged. For example, A may very well sell his motorbike valued at Rs. 50,000/- for a sum of Rs. 10,000/-

Law leaves the party to make their own bargain. Inadequate consideration would not invalidate an agreement but inadequate consideration raise suspicion over free will and could be taken into account by the court in deciding whether the consent of the promisor was freely given. (Topic of free consent dealt with separately)

(vii) The performance of an act by a person what he is legally bound to perform, cannot be consideration for a contract. For example, a promise to pay money to a witness for giving evidence is void. The witness is legally bound to furnish evidence and hence there is no consideration.

But where a person promises to do more than he is legally bound to do is a good consideration. For example, Police is bound to maintain law and order and protect person and property. But where police provides stationary guard at request of owner of property on agreed price for such service. It was held that the promise to pay the amount was not without consideration. The police, no doubt, were bound to afford protection, but they had discretion as to the form it should take. The undertaking to provide more protection than what they deemed to be necessary was a consideration for the promise of reward.

(viii) Consideration must not be unlawful, immoral, or opposed to public policy.

(ix) Consideration may be positive or negative. Consideration is positive when some act needs to be done. It is negative when some act is to be purposely omitted.

6.2. Agreement without Consideration

The general rule is that an agreement without consideration is void. However, there are certain exceptions to the general rule. They are -

1. Agreement on account of Natural love and affection:

Such an agreement must be -

(a) In writing and registered,

(b) Made on account of natural love and affection,

(c) Between parties standing in a near relation to each other.

In aforementioned conditions, an agreement is enforceable by law even without consideration.

2. Compensation paid for past voluntary services:

Such an agreement must be -

(a) A promise to compensate,

(b) Wholly or in part,

(c) Person rendered services to the promisor,

(d) Such service was rendered voluntarily.

That is, a promise to compensate wholly or in part for past voluntary services rendered by someone to promisor does not require consideration for being enforced. However the past services must have been rendered voluntarily to the promisor. Further the promisor must have been in existence at that time and he must have intended to compensate.

3. Promise to pay debts barred by limitation:

Such an agreement must be -

(a) A promise, made in writing,

(b) Signed by the person to be charged therewith, or by his agent,

(c) To pay, wholly or in part,

(d) A time barred debt.

That is, Where there is a promise in writing to pay a debt, which was barred by limitation, is valid without consideration. The law of limitations prescribes time within which an action must be initiated, after the lapse of which the same is called barred by time or limitation.

4. Creation of Agency:

By law, no consideration is necessary to create an agency. An "agent" is a person employed to do any act for another or to represent another in dealings with third persons.

5. Gifts actually made

In case of completed gifts, no consideration is necessary.

7. CAPACITY TO CONTRACT

We already know that the parties to a contract must be competent, that is, they must have the capacity to contract. The question, now, is who is competent to contract?

Law states that every person is competent to contract who is of the age of majority according to the law to which he is subject, and who is of sound mind, and is not disqualified from contracting by any law to which he is subject. That is, person is competent to contract if he -

(a) has attained the age of majority,

(b) is of sound mind, and

(c) is not otherwise disqualified from contracting.

7.1. AGE OF MAJORITY

Law states that every domiciled Indian attains majority on the completion of 18 years of age. But what is a person below the age of majority makes an agreement. The effect of such an agreement are as follows -

(i) An agreement entered into by a minor is altogether void.

An agreement entered into by a minor is void ab initio, that is, void from its inception. The question of its enforceability does not arise. Unless all the parties to an agreement are competent to contract, the agreement would be void. The main reason is that a minor is incapable of performing his part of the contract imposing a legal obligation.

(ii) Minor can be a beneficiary:

A minor, though incompetent to contract, make the other party bound towards himself. For example, a promissory note duly executed in favour of a minor is not void. Minor can enforce the same as he may accept a benefit.

Similarly, a minor cannot become partner in a partnership firm. However with the consent of all the partners, he may be admitted to the benefits of partnership.

(iii) Minor can always plead minority.

Minor can always plead minority. Even if a minor had stated himself an adult and entered into an agreement, and also received certain benefit out of the same; he may at a later stage plead minority and that the agreement is void. Thus, the law of estoppel is not available against a minor.

Say, for example, any money advanced to a minor cannot be recovered as he can plead minority and that the contract is void. Even if there had been false representation at the time of borrowing that he was a major, the amount lent to him cannot be recovered.

If a minor had obtained payment fraudulently by concealing his age, he may be compelled to restore the payment. But he cannot be compelled for an identical sum as it would amount to enforcing a void contract.

(iv) Minor cannot ratify his agreement even after attaining the age of majority.

A minor on his attaining majority cannot validate any agreement which was entered into when he was minor. Such a ratification amounts to agreement without consideration and is void. For example, Where A aged 19 executes a fresh promissory note in lieu of promissory note executed for a loan executed when A was 17 years of age (minor as per law). The fresh promissory note is without consideration and hence void.

(v) Liability for necessaries.

A person who supplied necessaries of life to a minor or his family, is entitled to be reimbursed from the properties of a minor. But this is not a contractual obligation in strict sense, but an obligation resembling a contract (also called Quasi contract). Necessaries of life include food, clothing, education etc. It is necessary to note that the minor is not personally liable but the cost of necessaries may be recovered from the estate of the minor.

(vi) Contract by guardian are valid.

A valid contract can be entered into with the guardian on behalf of the minor. The guardian must be competent to make the contract and the contract should be for the benefit of the minor. It is important to note in certain cases permission of Court is required to enter into such contracts. Such as for sale of immovable property of a minor, the guardian must seek permission of the court for a valid transaction.

7.2. SOUND MIND

A person must be of "sound mind" to be able to enter into a valid contract. The term "sound mind" is used in legal sense and in ordinary sense. Legally, a person is considered to be of sound mind if he at the time of entering into a contract is capable of understanding it and forming a rational judgment as to its effect upon his interest.

A person who is of unsound mind but occasionally of sound mind can enter into a contact when he is in sound mind. Similarly, a person who is generally of sound mind, but occasionally of unsound mind cannot enter into a contract when he is of unsound mind. Thus, the period of lucidity is crucial in deciding competency of party in such cases. Similarly, a person while drunk may not be competent at times. The test of competency is -

capable of understanding the contract

form a rational judgment as to its effect upon his interest

In short, whether the person is able to understand the implications of the contract in question.

Thus, if you are a bar tender and a person has already drunk enough to lose his sense but presses for another drink. Its better not to serve him as he cannot be compelled by law to pay. There can be no valid contract after he lost his sense. Neither the case is covered under supply for necessaries.

The effect of an agreement with an unsound is same as that of a minor.

7.3. NOT DISQUALIFIED BY LAW

At times, a person may be disqualified by law to enter into contract either wholly or partially.

For example, an alien enemy, during war cannot enter into a contract with an Indian subject. This disability to an alien enemy arises on account of public policy. Also, Statutory corporations or Municipal bodies cannot enter into contracts on matters which are beyond their statutory powers or ultra vires the memorandum or articles through which they are created.

8. FREE CONSENT

Two or more persons are said to consent when they agree upon the same thing in the same sense. This is called "consensus-ad-idem", that is, identity of minds.

Absence of "consensus-ad-idem" arises when there is error on the part of the parties regarding -

(a) nature of transaction, or

(b) identity of party, or

(c) subject matter of agreement.

In such cases there would be no consent. For example, where parties refer to a name of a ship in the contract but each of them had a different ship in mind though of same name, there is no identity of minds and hence there is no consent.

The consent referred above must be a "free consent". Consent is free when it is not caused by -

(a) Coercion,

(b) Undue influence,

(c) Fraud,

(d) Misrepresentation, or

(e) Mistake

Consent is said to be so caused when it would not have been given but for the existence of such coercion, undue influence, fraud, misrepresentation or mistake.

It is important to note here itself that when the consent is caused by mistake, the agreement is void, but when caused by any other of the aforementioned factors it is voidable. Now, we will discuss each of these elements.

8.1. Coercion

"Coercion" is the committing, or threatening to commit, any act forbidden by the Indian Penal Code, or the unlawful detaining, or threatening to detain, any property, to the prejudice of any person whatever, with the intention of causing any person to enter into an agreement.

Thus, coercion is -

(i) Commit, or threat to commit

(ii) Act forbidden by IPC or

(iii) Unlawful detention, or threat to detain

(iv) Property

(v) Prejudice of any person

(vi) With intention of causing any person to enter into an agreement.

For example, A says to B 'I shall not return the documents of title relating to your property, unless you agree to sell your house to me for Rs. 5 Lacs. B replies, "All right, I shall sell my house to you for Rs. 5 Lacs, do not detain documents of title." A has employed coercion.

Here A cannot therefore enforce the contract. But B can do so. This is because an agreement induced by coercion is not void but merely voidable at the option of the party coerced.

8.2. Undue influence

A contract is said to be induced by "undue influence" where the relations subsisting between the parties are such that one of the parties is in a position to dominate the will of the other and uses that position to obtain an unfair advantage over the other. A person is deemed to be in a position to dominate the will of another where he holds a real or apparent authority over the other or where he stands in a fiduciary relation to the other; or where he makes a contract with a person whose mental capacity is temporarily or permanently affected by reason of age, illness, or mental or bodily distress.

Thus, the essential ingredients of undue influence are -

(i) One party in position to dominate the will of the other

(ii) Such domination is presumed where one party -

(a) holds real or apparent authority over the other or

(b) stands in a fiduciary relation to the other

(iii) makes a contract with a person whose mental capacity is temporarily or permanently affected by reason of age, illness, or mental or bodily distress.

(iv) Position is used to obtain an unfair advantage over other.

Example where one person may be able to dominate the will of the other are -

(a) A father is able to dominate will of financially dependent son.

(b) A solicitor can dominate the will of the client.

(c) A doctor can dominate the will of his patient having protracted illness.

(d) A trustee can dominate the will of the beneficiary.

When the transaction appears, on the face of it, to be unconscionable, the burden of proof that there is no undue influence in an agreement would be on the person who is in a position to dominate the will of the other. This is to ensure that the party in dominant position acts in good faith.

Examples of agreements where undue influence has been exercised are -

(i) An old person making a gift of whole of his property to his spiritual advisor without even having regard to his own physiological and medical needs.

(ii) An illiterate pardanashin lady makes a contract while acting on advice and complete belief of manager of her estate, which is apparently more beneficial to the manager and detrimental to the interest of the lady.

8.3. Fraud

In common parlance, Fraud means to cheat by intentionally misleading a person. In law, "Fraud" means and includes any of the following acts committed by a party to a contract, or with his connivance, or by his agent, with intent to deceive another party thereto or his agent, or to induce him to enter into the contract :-

(a) the suggestion, as a fact, of that which is not true, by one who does not believe it to be true;

(b) the active concealment of a fact by one having knowledge or belief of the fact;

(c) a promise made without any intention of performing it;

(d) any other act fitted to deceive;

(e) any such act or omission as the law specially declares to be fraudulent.

Intention is very important aspect of fraud. Without intent, there can be no fraud although there can an honest misrepresentation of fact. Examples of fraud are -

(i) A company issues prospectus containing misstatement having complete knowledge of the same. Any person who purchases shares on the faith of such misstatement can repudiate the contract on the ground of fraud.

(ii) B discovered an ore mine in A's estate. B conceals the information about the mine. A in ignorance agrees to sell the estate to B at a price that is grossly undervalued had mine been known. The contract would be voidable of A's option on the ground of fraud.

(iii) Buying goods with the intention of not paying the price is an act of fraud.

A seller of a property is under a duty to disclose any material defect in the property. Concealing the information would be an act of fraud.

As a general rule, mere silence is no fraud. But where it is the duty of the person keeping silence to speak, or unless his silence is in itself equivalent to speech, Silence may amount to fraud. Consider following examples -

(i) B is A's daughter and has just come of age. Here, the relation between the parties would make it A's duty to tell B if the horse is unsound.

(ii) B says to A - "If you do not deny it, I shall assume that the horse is sound". A says nothing. Here A's silence is equivalent to speech.

(iii) A and B, being traders, enter upon a contract. A has private information of a change in prices which would affect B's willingness to proceed with the contract. A is not bound to inform B.

8.4. Misrepresentation

"Misrepresentation" means and includes-

(1) the positive assertion, in a manner not warranted by the information of the person making it, of that which is not true, though he believes it to be true;

(2) any breach of duty which, without an intent to deceive, gains an advantage to the person committing it, or any one claiming under him, by misleading another to his prejudice or to the prejudice of any one claiming under him;

(3) causing, however innocently, a party to an agreement to make a mistake as to the substance of the thing which is the subject of the agreement.

Thus, "Misrepresentation" means making an assertion of an untrue statement honestly believing it to be true. Thus, misrepresentation does not involve deception or deceit. A contract person misled may A contract which is hit by misrepresentation can be avoided by the person who has been misled.

For example, A makes the statement on an information derived, not directly from C but from M. B applies for shares on the faith of the statement which turns out to be false. The statement amounts to misrepresentation, because the information received second-hand did not warrant A to make the positive statement to B

To understand the difference between fraud and misrepresentation, take this example. The promoters of a company mentioned in their prospectus that they had a right to run steam powered tramway. A person purchased shares on the basis of the said statement. But the company could not get the permission of board of trade to run steam powered engines. The person brought action for fraud against the promoters. The promoters plead that since they had a right under the Act of parliament for using steam, they had presumed, they would also get the consent of Board of trade. The Court held that there was no deceit.

8.5. Consequence of Coercion, Undue Influence. Fraud or Misrepresentation on a Contract

As a general rule, a contract in which a party's consent is caused by coercion, undue influence, fraud or misrepresentation is voidable at the option of the party whose consent was so obtained. That is the effected party may compel its performance in the court of law, but successfully defend a similar legal action by the opposite party.

For example, where A intending to deceive B, falsely represents that 500 tons of sugar are made annually at A's factory, and thereby induces B to buy the factory. The contract is voidable at the option of B.

In cases of Fraud or misrepresentation, the effected party may insist that the contract shall be performed, and that he shall be put in the position in which he would have been if the representations made had been true.

For example, A fraudulently informs B that his estate is free from encumbrance, therefore B buys the estate. But the estate is subject to mortgage. B may avoid the contract or insist on the debt being redeemed and mortgage being released.

Exception

There are three exceptions to the aforementioned general rule. Firstly, where it is possible to discover the truth with ordinary diligence, and though the consent might have been obtained by misrepresentation or silence, fraudulent then the contract is not voidable.

For example, A, by a misrepresentation, leads B erroneously to believe that 500 tons of sugar are made annually at A's factory. B examines the accounts of the factory, which show that only 400 tons of sugar have been made. After this B buys the factory. The contract is not voidable on account of A's misrepresentation.

Note, that this exception is limited to cases of misrepresentation and fraud by silence. And cases of active fraudulent statements are not covered there-in.

Secondly, where a party to contract perpetrates fraud or misrepresentation, but the other party is not misled by such fraud or misrepresentation, then the contract cannot be avoided by the latter.

For example, a used car seller deliberately conceals a scratch in order that the buyer may not discover it even if he inspects the goods, but the buyer in fact does not make any inspection at all, the buyer cannot avoid the contract as his consent has not resulted from fraud. That he is in-fact not deceived by the seller.

Thirdly, in cases of undue influence, where the effected party has received any benefit under the contract, the Court may set aside the contract upon such terms and conditions as it may seem just.

For example, A, a money-lender, advances Rs. 100 to B, an agriculturist, and, by undue influence, induces B to execute a bond for Rs. 200 with interest at 6 per cent. per month. The Court may set the bond aside, ordering B to repay the Rs. 100 with such interest as may seem just. The whole idea here is to set thing right rather than tilt the balance other way round.

It is important to note that where a contract is voidable and the party entitled to avoid it decides to do so by rescinding it, he must restore any benefit which he might have received from the other party. He cannot avoid the contract and at the same time enjoy the benefit under the rescinded/avoided contract.

8.6. Mistake

Mistake means unintentional error. Where both the parties to an agreement are under a mistake as to a matter of fact essential to the agreement, the agreement is void. It is so because Mistake vitiates Consent. Such an agreement cannot be enforced at all.

To vitiate an agreement, the characteristics of a mistake must be as follows -

(a) Mistake must be of a fact.

(b) Mistake should not be of a law.

(c) The fact mistaken be essential to the agreement.

(d) Mistake should be mutual, that is, of both the parties and not merely a unilateral mistake.

(e) Mistake as to foreign law is deemed to be a mistake of fact.

For example, A agrees to sell to B a specific cargo of goods supposed to be on its way from England to Bombay. It turns out that, before the day of the bargain, the ship conveying the cargo had been cast away and the goods lost. Neither party was aware of the facts. The agreement is void.

Where two persons enter into an agreement believing wrongly that a particular debt is not barred by law of limitation, then the contract is valid because there is no mistake of fact but of law only.

Where A agrees to purchase from B 18 carat gold thinking it to be pure gold, but B was not instrumental for creating such an impression. The contract is a valid one. As A's mistake is a unilateral one.

9. LAWFUL OBJECT AND CONSIDERATION

Contractual freedom is not absolute. There are certain limitations. For example, Two persons agree to rob a bank and share the loot. Such an agreement is unlawful as its object is unlawful.

Object of a contract is the reason behind a contract, while consideration refers to what one party gives and other receives. Generally, they are intermingled in a contract.

As far as what are lawful object and consideration, the law is that the consideration or object of an agreement is lawful, unless -

(a) it is forbidden by law; or

(b) is of such a nature that, if permitted, it would defeat the provisions of any law; or

(c) is fraudulent; or

(d) involves or implies injury to the person or property of another, or

(e) the Court regards it as immoral, or opposed to public policy.

Thus, law has defined lawful in negative manner. That is, it chalks our instances as to what cannot be the object or consideration of a valid agreement.

9.1. Forbidden by law

Forbidden by law means acts that are punishable under any law, that is, statute, enactment or rules made thereunder. If the object or consideration of any agreement is forbidden by law, the same is void.

For example, an agreement to buy-sell property which parties know to be stolen is void. As dealings in stolen property is an offence punishable under IPC.

9.2. If permitted, defeat the provisions of any law

Agreement, whose object or consideration is aimed at defeating any provision of law, is void.

For example, A, owner of land, is in land revenue arrears. His land was attached and ordered for auction. A makes an agreement with B, that B shall purchase the land for revenue's sake and re-convey it to A on receipt of purchase money. The agreement is void as it is intended to defeat the legal provision that prohibits the owner from purchasing the land sold due to his default.

Similarly, an agreement by a Hindu father to give his son in adoption in exchange of annual allowance is in violation of Hindu Law.

9.3. Fraudulent

There is a difference between consent caused by fraud (refer to free consent) and Fraudulent object or consideration. Here, an agreement is fraudulent, when it is aimed at cheating a third person.

For example, A & B are partners in a firm. They agree to defraud a Government department by submitting a tender in the individual name and not in the firm name. This agreement is void as it is a fraud on the Government department.

9.4. Involves injury to person or property of another

Injury means infringement of a legal right. An agreement whose object or consideration involves injury to a person of his property, is void.

For example, A agrees to buy a house from B although A knows that B has already executed an agreement to sell in favour of C, which is still in force. Since, the intention of the agreement is to injure C, the agreement is void.

Similarly, where A agrees to print a book in B's name, which had already been published by X, the agreement is void. It is not only in violation of the Copyright Act but also intends to cause injury to the property of another.

9.5. Immoral

Immoral means violating principles of right and wrong or not adhering to ethical or moral principles. An agreement with immoral object or consideration is void.

For example, an agreement in consideration of future illicit cohabitation between the parties is void.

Also, where A lends money to X, a married woman, to enable her to obtain a divorce from her husband. He also promised to marry her after divorce. It was held that A was not entitled to recover the amount from X as the agreement was against good morals.

9.6. Opposed to public policy

If the object or consideration of an agreement are opposed to public policy, the agreement is void and unenforceable.

Policy means a line of argument rationalizing the course of action. Any institution or association may have its policy, but the term is generally used for the government. Public policy is sum total of ideas, thoughts and visions for a good and orderly society. But what is and what is not a part of public policy is a difficult question. Public policy has to be developed with circumspection. It has been described as "an unruly horse, which if not properly bridled, may carry its rider he knows not where". The general theme is that, having regard to times and circumstances, whatever constitutes injury to public interest and welfare is regarded as opposed to public policy.

But there are certain activities that are regarded as against public policy. Some of them are as follows -

(a) Trading with enemy

Any trading or business activity with a person who owes allegiance to a country with whom India is at war is void. As such a trade would be against the interest of the people and Government of India.

Also, any agreement made prior to war during peace times would be suspended automatically and cannot be carried on further until hostilities come to an end.

(b) Stifling prosecution

An agreement to stifle or prevent illegally any prosecution is void. That is, felony cannot be traded. It amounts to perversion or abuse of justice. But, if the offence is compoundable, the same may be compounded as per law.

(c) Maintenance and Champerty

Maintenance means promotion of litigation in which the litigant has no interest. Champerty means bargain whereby one party agrees to assist the other in recovering property with a view to sharing the profit of litigation.

Agreements for maintenance and champerty are not opposed to public policy in India. But where such advances are made by way of gambling in litigation, the agreement to share the subject of litigation is certainly opposed to public policy and therefore is void.

(d) Interference with course of law and justice

Any agreement with the object of inducing a judicial or administrative officer of the state to act corruptly or not impartially is void.

(e) Marriage brokerage contract

An agreement to negotiate a marriage for reward is void. Such marriage brokerage contracts are opposed to public policy.

(f) Sale of public offices

While appointing a person to certain important and high public office, merit alone should be the criteria. Any attempt to influence should be seen as an act opposed to public policy. Thus, money consideration in the matter amounts to sale of public office.

For example, A agrees to pay money to B, a public servant, if he opts for voluntary retirement so that A may secure appointment. The agreement amounts to sale of public office.

Similarly, an agreement to procure a public recognition like Padma Vibhushan for reward is void.

10. AGREEMENT EXPRESSLY DECLARED TO BE VOID

There are certain agreements which the law regard as void, such as minor's agreement, or agreement under mutual mistake of fact, or agreement without consideration, or whose object or consideration is unlawful.

Apart from those discussed earlier, there is a list of agreements, specifically enumerated in the Indian Contract Act, that are void. They are as follows -

10.1. Where consideration is unlawful in part

If any part of a single consideration for one or more objects, or any one or any part of any one of several considerations for a single object, is unlawful, the agreement is void.

The above language of the law may appear technical. But it is corollary to previously discussed unlawful objects and considerations. Where object or consideration of an agreement is unlawful, but merely in part, the law examines whether the legal part can be separated from the illegal part. If yes, then the legal part is given effect while the illegal is rejected. But where no such separation is possible, the agreement is altogether void.

For example, where A promises to manage B's business, manufacturing of sugar, and also illegal smuggling of alcohol. B promises to pay to A a monthly salary of Rs. 10,000. The agreement is void.

But if B had agreed to pay Rs. 5000 for sugar business and another Rs. 5000 for alcohol smuggling. The agreement would be valid for management of sugar business for a monthly salary of Rs 5000.

10.2. Agreement in restraint of marriage

Every agreement in restraint of the marriage of any person, other than a minor, is void. So if a major person agrees for good consideration not to marry, the promise is not binding.

10.3. Agreement in restraint of trade

Every agreement by which any one is restrained from exercising a lawful profession, trade or business of any kind, is to that extent void. The object of this law is to protect trade. The restraint, even if it is partial, will make the agreement void.

For example, A, a shop keeper, in a particular locality agrees to pay B his business rival certain compensation, if B closes his business in that locality the agreement is void.

However, there are certain exceptions to the general rule based on the principle of fairness. They are as follows -

(i) <u>Sale of goodwill</u>

An agreement by a person who sells the goodwill of a business, not to carry on a similar business within specified local limits so long as the buyer carries on a similar business, is valid provided that the restrictions are reasonable.

(ii) <u>Partnership Act</u>

Under the law of Partnership, partners may agree not to carry on any other business during continuance of partnership. This restriction may be absolute so that partners remain focused on partnership business

Also, an outgoing partner may be restrained by agreement from carrying on competing business for a reasonable time or within specific locality. It is worth noting that this restriction can only be partial and with respect to competing business only

Similarly, on dissolution of partnership firm, the partners may agree that one or more of them will not carry on business similar to that of the dissolved partnership for a reasonable time or within specific locality. This restriction, again, cannot be absolute.

(iii) <u>Exclusive Dealing Agreements</u>

Law even provides for exclusive dealing agreements. Such as, An agreement that during a term, entire production of a factory will be sold exclusively to one dealer, is not in restraint of trade.

Similarly, an agreement of service through which an employee commits not to compete with his employer is not in restraint of trade. Say, A, a Doctor, employs B as his assistant under the condition that B shall not practice as an independent Doctor during the period of his employment. The agreement is valid.

(iv) <u>Trade Unions</u>

Trade unions may adopt reasonable covenants for regulation of business. For example. Union of traders may agree that sellers shall not sell a particular product below a particular price.

10.4. Agreement in restraint of legal proceedings

An agreement, which restricts a party absolutely from enforcing his rights in respect of any contract or which limits the time within which the right may be enforced, is void to that extent.

However, there is an important exception to the rule, that is, arbitration. Parties may agree that any dispute between them, whether present or future, shall be referred to arbitration. Such an agreement must be in writing and signed by the parties. Such an agreement bars civil litigation before a court or tribunal.

It is important to note that initiation of a criminal action for a non-compoundable offence cannot be restrained by way of agreement.

10.5. Uncertain Agreements

Agreements, the meaning of which is not certain, or capable of being made certain, are void. But where the meaning is capable of being made certain, then the agreement is valid.

For example where A enters into an agreement to supply 100 tons of oil, the agreement is not valid as the meaning of it is uncertain since the type of oil is not known. But if A is a dealer of coconut oil only, then the meaning of the agreement is capable of being ascertained from the circumstances surrounding the promise. Such an agreement shall be valid.

10.6. Wagering agreement

Agreements by way of wager are void. Wager is a promise to give money or money's worth upon determination or ascertainment of an uncertain event. It is an agreement by which two or more parties agree that a certain sum of money, or thing, shall be paid or delivered to any of them, on the happening or not happening of an uncertain event. The essence of wagering agreement is where there are two parties, one wins, the other loses upon an uncertain event taking place in which neither of them has legitimate interest. That is -

(i) Two parties

(ii) Mutual chances of gain and loss

(iii) Uncertain Event

(iv) No interest other than stake

(v) Neither party to have control over the event

For example A agrees to pay Rs. 500/- to B if it rains and similarly B agrees to pay A if it does not. This is a wagering agreement as neither has control over the event. But where one of the parties has control over the event, the agreement is valid.

The law provides for two exceptions of the rule. Firstly, Horse racing tickets, where Rs 500 or more is to be awarded to the winner, are valid.

Secondly, Speculative transactions. Speculation means the act or practice of buying land, goods, shares, etc., in expectation of selling at a higher price, or of selling with the expectation of repurchasing at a lower price. It is trading on anticipated fluctuations in price, as distinguished from trading in which the profit expected is the difference between the retail and wholesale prices, or prices in different markets.

There are two elements of a speculative transaction -

(a) Mutual intention of parties to acquire or deliver goods and not mere exchange of difference in price.

(b) Undertaking of risk arising from change of prices.

In wager, risk is the only element without ever intention to deliver goods. Wagering agreement is void, speculative transactions are valid.

It is often difficult to distinguish between the two. For example, A enters into a agreement with B to buy 100 bags of cement at Rs. 400/- per bag for delivery after 6 months. After 6 months, the prices are Rs. 500/-. A may -

(a) Take delivery of 100 bags on payment at the rate of Rs. 400/- and sell it to some other buyer at prevailing rates in the market and make profit, or

(b) Simply collect the difference of Rs. 10,000/- at rate of Rs. 100/- per bag.

Similarly, if the price falls to Rs. 350/-, A may -

(a) Take delivery of 100 bags on payment at the rate of Rs. 400/- and sell it to some other buyer at prevailing rates in the market and incur loss, or

(b) Pay the difference of Rs. 5000/- at rate of Rs. 50/- per bag.

In the above example, if the original intention of the parties was to settle the difference in price only, then the agreement is by way of wager, and thus void. But if the original intention was delivery of the goods, the transaction is one of speculation and a valid one.

Further, Insurance contract are in their nature speculative. To avoid them from becoming a wager, law provides that the person seeking insurance must have insurable interest in the subject matter. Insurable interest means interest in the survival or preservation of the person or the thing. That is, if death of a person or destruction of the object is detrimental to a person, he has an insurable interest in the person or thing. Thus, one can insure one's own life, life of a family member, one's own car. But not one' neighbour's car. Unless for some reason, an insurable interest may be established, an insurance policy so taken will be void.

It is also worth noting that at times when a bet is placed, parties may agree that the amount of bet be placed with a neutral third party (stakeholder). But even such an arrangement does not make wager a valid contract. A winner cannot compel the stakeholder to deliver him the award.

Collateral transactions

Transactions collateral to, though independent of, wager are valid. Wagering agreements are void and unenforceable in nature, but not forbidden by law. The test of validly of a collateral transaction is whether the main transaction is illegal or legal but void. If the main transaction is illegal, the collateral transaction are also invalid.

For example, A lends money to B, to pay off the debts arising out of a wagering agreement or bet. Though, B makes payment over a void agreement, and A has knowledge of the same, but since the agreement between A and B is collateral to wager and not to an illegal agreement or wager in itself, A can recover the loan from B.

11. PERFORMANCE OF CONTRACT

A contract being an agreement enforceable by law, creates a legal obligation, which subsists until discharged. Performance of the promise or promises remaining to be performed is the principal and most usual mode of discharge. This chapter deals with -

(a) who must perform his obligation;

(b) what should be the mode of performance; and

(c) what shall be the consequences of non performance.

The parties to a contract must either perform, or offer to perform, their respective promises, unless such performance is dispensed with or excused under the law.

Performance of one's part is primary obligation under the contract. Unless, the party is treated as having been absolved under the provisions of any law or by the conduct of the other party, the performance is neither excused nor dispensed with.

11.1. By Whom a Contract may be Performed

The promise under a contract can be performed by any one of the following:

(i) Promisor himself

Invariably the promise has to be performed by the promisor himself. Particularly, where the contract is entered into for performance of personal skills, or diligence or personal confidence, it becomes absolutely necessary that the promisor performs it himself.

(ii) Agent

Where personal consideration is not the foundation of a contract, the promisor can employ a competent person to perform it.

(iii) Representatives

Generally upon the death of promisor, the legal representatives of the deceased are bound by the promise unless it is a promise for performance involving personal skill or ability of the promisor. However the liability of the legal representative is limited to the value of property inherited by him from the promisor.

(iv) Third Person

At times, a total stranger to a contract may be directed to perform the promise. In such case, of a promisee accepts performance from a third party he cannot afterwards enforce it against the promisor.

(v) Joint promisors

Where two or more persons jointly promise, the promise must be performed jointly unless a contrary intention appears from the contract.

The above rules may appear tedious. But can be understood with the help of following examples -

(i) A promises to pay B a sum of money. A may perform this promise, either by personally paying the money to B or by causing it to be paid to B by another. And if A dies before the time appointed for payment, his representatives must perform the promise, or employ some proper person to do so, to the extent they have inherited from A.

(ii) A promises B to pay Rs. 1000/- on delivery of certain item. A may perform this promise either himself or causing someone else to pay the money to B. If A dies before the time appointed for payment, his representative must pay the money or employ some other person to pay the money. If B dies before the time appointed for the delivery of goods, B's representative shall be bound to deliver the goods to A and A is bound to pay Rs. 1000/- to B's representative. (Note – After death of a party, even the representatives may with mutual consent of the other alter or vary the terms of contract or discharge its performance altogether).

(iii) A promises to paint a picture for B for a certain price. A must perform this promise personally. He cannot employ some other painter to paint the picture on his behalf. If A dies before painting the picture, the contract cannot be enforced either by A's representative or by B.

(iv) A delivered certain goods to B who promised to pay Rs. 5000/-. Later on B expresses his inability to clear the dues. C, who is known to B, pays Rs. 2000/- to A on behalf of B, although without disclosing it to B. Now A can sue B only for the balance and not for the whole amount.

(v) A, B and C jointly promise to pay D 3,000 rupees. D may compel either A or B or C to pay him 3,000 rupees.

(vi) A, B and C jointly promise to pay D the sum of 3,000 rupees. C is compelled to pay the whole. A is insolvent, but his assets are sufficient to pay one-half of his debts. C is entitled to receive 500 rupees from A's estate and 1,250 rupees from B.

11.2. Effects of Refusal to Accept Offer of Performance

In a contract, parties must offer performance of their part. This offer of performance is known as 'tender'. For a valid tender, following conditions are a must -

(a) Offer of performance is unconditional.

(b) It is made at a proper time and place.

(c) Person to whom it is made has a reasonable opportunity to ascertain that the person by whom it is made is able and willing to do, what he is bound to under the contract.

(d) If the offer is to deliver any thing, then the promisee must have a reasonable opportunity to ascertain that the thing offered is the thing that the promisor is bound to deliver.

Where a promisee refuses to accept a valid offer or tender of performance by the promisor then the promisor is not responsible for non performance. And he does not forfeit his rights under the contract.

11.3. Effect of a Refusal of a Party to Perform Promise

When a party to a contract has refused to perform, or disabled himself from performing, his promise in its entirety, the promisee may put an end to the contract, unless he has signified, by words or conduct, his acquiescence in its continuance. Thus, the aggrieved party has following two options -

(a) Terminate the contract, or

(b) Indicate by words or conduct that he is interested in its continuance.

If the promisee puts an end to the contract, he is bound to return the benefit received under the contract and is entitled to receive compensation for the breach.

11.4. Performance of Reciprocal Promise

At times, a contract may consist of Reciprocal promises, that is, promises from both the sides to perform some act in present or future.

For example, A promises to sell 100 bags of wheat to B and B promises to pay the price on delivery. This contract consists of two reciprocal promises, that are consideration for one another.

Order of Performance of reciprocal promises

The rules pertaining to order of performance of reciprocal promises are as follows -

(i) <u>Simultaneous performance</u>

When a contract consists of reciprocal promises to be simultaneously performed, no promisor need perform his promise unless the promisee is ready and willing to perform his reciprocal promise.

For example, A and B contract that A shall deliver goods to B to be paid for by B on delivery. A need not deliver the goods, unless B is ready and willing to pay for the goods on delivery. B need not pay for the goods, unless A is ready and willing to deliver them on payment.

Similarly, A and B contract that A shall deliver goods to B at a price to be paid by instalments, the first instalment to be paid on delivery. A need not deliver, unless B is ready and willing to pay the first instalment on delivery. B need, not pay the first instalment, unless A is ready and willing to deliver the goods on payment of the first instalment.

(ii) Where the order is expressly fixed

Where the order of performance is expressly fixed, the promise must be performed in that order only.

For example, Where A promises to build a house for B and B promises to pay after construction. A must perform his promise before, A can compel B to make payment. A's performance of the promise is a condition precedent to B performing his part.

(iii) Implication by Nature of the transaction

Where a contract does not spell out order of performance, reciprocal promises shall be performed in the order which the nature of the transaction requires.

For example, A and B contract that A shall make over his stock-in-trade to B at a fixed price, and B promises to give security for the payment of the money. A's promise need not be performed until the security is given. The reason is that the from the nature of transaction, it can be gathered that security must precede delivery.

12. IMPOSSIBILITY OF PERFORMANCE

An agreement to do an act impossible in itself is void. A contract to do an act which, after the contract is made, becomes impossible, or, by reason of some event which the promisor could not prevent, unlawful, becomes void when the act becomes impossible or unlawful.

12.1. Impossibility existing at the time of contract

If performance of an agreement is impossible at the inception itself, the agreement is void. It is immaterial that the parties had the knowledge of impossibility or not. But where the promisor knew the performance to be impossible or unlawful, or might have known with reasonable diligence, and promisee did not know to be impossible or unlawful, he must make compensation to the promisee for any loss sustained due to non-performance of the promise.

12.2. Supervening impossibility

Supervening impossibility refers to the condition where the agreement is valid at the inception, but subsequent events or change in circumstances, beyond contemplation of the parties, has rendered its performance impossible or unlawful. In such cases, the contract is rendered void.

Some examples of Supervening impossibility are as follows -

(i) Accidental destruction of the subject matter of the contract

For example, A hires B's wedding hall for A's son's wedding on a certain date. Before the said date, the hall is destroyed by earthquake. The contract is rendered void because of the destruction of the subject matter.

(ii) Non-occurrence of a contemplated event

For example, A hires B's house on rent for specific time period to witness a religious procession. The purpose is disclosed to B. But the said procession is cancelled. A neither takes possession of the house nor pays the rent. Since the foundation of the contract has failed, A cannot be compelled to pay the rent.

(iii) Incapacity to perform a contract of personal services

Where the contract involves performance of the promise by the promisor using his own skill, promisor's disability, incapacity or illness amounts to supervening impossibility.

(iv) Change in law

At times, change in law may render the performance of a contract impossible. For example, a subsequent law may altogether prohibit the act which forms the basis of contract.

For example, A and B enter into partnership business for sale of lottery. Lottery is subsequently banned by the State. The partnership agreement becomes void.

(v) Outbreak of war

Out break of war may also affect performance of the contract. For example, agreement between individuals of two nations for supply of goods for a price becomes void on the outbreak of war between the two nations.

12.3. What would not constitute ground of impossibility

Some examples of situations that may appear but are not covered under supervening impossibility are as follows -

(a) A promised to B that he would arrange for B's marriage with his daughter. A could not persuade his daughter to marry B. B sued A. A pleaded impossibility. But it was held that there was no ground of impossibility. A should not have promised what he could not have accomplished. Further A had chosen to answer for voluntary act of his daughter and hence he was liable.

(b) The defendant agreed to supply specified quantity of 'cotton' manufactured by a mill with in a specified time to plaintiff. The defendant could not supply the material as the mill failed to make any production at that time. The defendant pleaded on the ground of impossibility. Held that contract was not performed by the defendant and he was responsible for the failure.

(c) A labour strike would not necessarily relieve a contractor from his obligation of unloading the ship within specified time.

To sum up, while judging the impossibility of performance issue, the Courts are very cautious since contracting parties often bind themselves to perform at any cost without proper regard to prevailing prices and market conditions. To uphold the defence of supervening impossibility, the event must be uncontemplated, compelling and beyond the control of parties.

13. APPROPRIATION OF PAYMENTS

Appropriation means distribution or allotment for a specific purpose. The question of appropriation arises when a person owes a number of debts to another person, and he makes payment. The question that arises is to which debt the payment has to be appropriated.

The rules of appropriation of payment are as follows -

(i) It is the primary right of Debtor (person making the payment) to make payment with express intimation that the payment is to be applied to the discharge of some particular debt. The Creditor is bound by such intimation.

(ii) If there is no express direction from the debtor, the intention of appropriation is to be gathered from the circumstances under which the payment is made. Here again, the creditor is bound by the circumstances and must appropriate the payment accordingly. For example, A owes B, among other debts, 1,000 rupees upon a promissory note which falls due on the first June. He owes B no other debt of that amount. On the first June A pays to B 1,000 rupees. The payment is to be applied to the discharge of that promissory note.

(iii) Where the debtor has omitted to intimate and there are no other circumstances indicating to which debt the payment is to be applied, the creditor may apply it at his discretion to any lawful debt actually due and payable to him from the debtor. In such a case, creditor may also appropriate the payment towards any debt the recovery of which is barred by limitation. Thus, if the debtor does not make any appropriation, at the time of payment, the right devolves on the creditor. Creditor may also appropriate the payment towards the outstanding interest, rather than principal amount.

(iv) When neither party makes an appropriation, the payment shall be applied in discharge of debts in order of time. Further If the debts are of equal standing, the payment shall be applied in discharge of each proportionately.

The lesson worth learning from the above rules is that while making payment, one must specifically state the debt to which the payment has to be appropriated.

14. CONTRACTS WHICH NEED NOT BE PERFORMED

Law states that if the parties to a contract agree to substitute a new contract for it or to rescind or alter it, the original contract need not be performed. Thus, A contract need not be performed under following circumstances – novation, rescission, alteration and remission.

14.1. Novation

Novation means substitution, that is, replacement of one obligation by another. Where a given contract is substituted by a new contract it is called Novation. On novation, the old contract ceases to be enforceable and need not be performed. Novation can take place with mutual consent. However novation can take place by substitution of new contract between the same parties or between different parties.

For example, A owes money to B under a contract. It is agreed between A, B and C that B shall thenceforth accept C as his debtor, instead of A. The old debt of A to B is at an end, and a new debt from C to B has been contracted.

14.2. Rescission

Recession means ceding back. In rescission, the old contract is cancelled and no new contract takes its place. Contract may be rescinded by mutual agreement of the parties or by implication of conduct. But is not a unilateral act. Once rescinded, parties are not obliged to perform their part under the contract.

14.3. Alteration

Where the contract is altered, the original contract is rescinded. Alteration involves changes in the terms of contract by mutual consent, without change of parties. Again, there can be no unilateral material alteration to a contract. Unilateral alteration is void.

14.4. Remission

Remission means waiver. Law provides that every promisee may dispense with or remit, wholly or in part, the performance of the promise made to him, or may extend the time for such performance, or may accept instead of it any satisfaction which he thinks fit. For example, A owes B Rs. 5000/-. A pays Rs. 2000/- to B, and B accepts it in satisfaction of the whole debt. The whole debt is discharged. The balance is deemed to be remitted.

Remission can be in following forms -

(i) Dispense with performance.

(ii) Remit, wholly or in part.

(iii) Extend Time.

(iv) Accept any other satisfaction.

Remission is a unilateral act of the promisee and does not require consideration. The provision is based on contractual nature of obligation and a person's right to determine for himself.

15. DISCHARGE OF A CONTRACT

A contract may be discharged in following ways -

(a) Performance

Performance may be actual or attempted, that is, a valid tender which is refused by the promisee.

(b) Mutual agreement

Contract may be discharged by mutual agreement in form of – novation, rescission or alteration.

(c) Remission

A promisee may remit performance of the promise by the promisor, wholly or in part.

(d) Impossibility of performance

Supervening impossibility of performance of a contract also discharge the parties of their liabilities.

(e) Lapse of time

Obligation under the contract must be performed within certain prescribed time. There is a time limit within which an action may brought before a Court of law. On lapse of such period, the action becomes barred by law of limitation. And the party erring need not perform his part.

(f) Operation of law

Where the promisor dies or goes insolvent there is a discharge by operation of law.

(g) Breach of contract

Breach of contract, actual breach or anticipatory, by one party discharges the other from performing his part of the contract.

(h) Refusal of reasonable facilities

If any promisee neglects or refuses to afford the promisor reasonable facilities, for the performance of his promise, the promisor is excused by such neglect or refusal as to any non-performance caused thereby. For example, A hires B to paint his house. But A does allow B to enter his house. B is discharged from performance.

16. BREACH OF CONTRACT

Breach means breaking of the rules. In respect of contract, breach means failure to perform what is required under the contract. Breach of contract is of two types – Anticipatory and Actual.

16.1. Anticipatory Breach of Contract

Where the promisor refuses to perform his obligation even before the specified time for performance and signifies his unwillingness, then there is an anticipatory breach.

For example, A engages services of B as his attendant for a 3 months tour at Rs. 5000/- per month starting from 1st June. However, A changes his mind before the date and informs B that his services are not required. This is anticipatory breach of contract.

In such cases, B may put an end to the contract even before the due date, 1st June, and he need not wait for the date meant for performance of the promise. B could also wait till the due date of performance before he puts an end to the contract.

The measure of damage depends upon the choice and circumstances. For example, A agrees to supply 10 bags of wheat to B at the rate of Rs. 2000/- on May 31st. However, A gives notice to B of his unwillingness to sell on May 15th. Price of wheat on 15th is Rs. 2200/-. If B repudiates that contract on 15th, he may recover damages of Rs. 2000/- (at the rate of Rs. 200/- per bag).

But if B waits till May 31st, and prices are Rs. 2250/-, he may recover damages of Rs. 2500/- (at the rate of Rs. 250/- per bag).

Alternatively, if B waits till May 31st, and prices are reduced to Rs. 2100/-, he may recover damages of Rs. 1000/- only (at the rate of Rs. 1000/- per bag). Thus, postponement of right to repudiate is not meant to give unfair advantage to the promisee.

16.2. Actual Breach of Contract

Where one of the parties breaches the contract by refusing to perform the promise on due date, it is known as actual breach of contract. In such a case the other party to contract obtains a right of action against the one who breached the contract.

16.3. Measurement of Damages

Where a party makes a breach of contract, he is liable to compensate the other party for the loss suffered on account of such breach. But a party is liable to compensate only for such loss, that is -

(i) Naturally arose in usual course of things from such breach or

(ii) Which the parties knew, when they made the contract, to be likely to result from the breach

Second category of damages are special damages and can be claimed only on previous notice. However no compensation is payable for any remote or any indirect loss.

For example, A is owner of a mill. The mill had to be stopped because of a broken crank shaft. A sends the crank shaft as a pattern for manufacturing a new one. Till the arrival of the new crank shaft, the mill could not be resumed. Hence, A incurred losses. However this position was not properly conveyed to the carrier. There were some delay on the part of the carrier in delivering the crank shaft to the manufacturer which in turn delayed the reopening of the mill. As a result, there were losses to the mill. A claimed compensation for loss in profit. But since A did not explain the peculiar position to the carrier that delay in delivering the crank shaft would delay resumption of the mill, and this would result in losses, his claim for special damages was rejected.

A similar example can be, in a case a tailor had given his sewing machine to railways to be delivered at a station as a consignment. He did not mention that any delay in delivering the sewing machine would result in damages for the business of the tailor as he had planned to do good business at the place proposed where a festival was to be held. The sewing machine was delivered after the festival was over. Held Railways were not responsible for the damages as the Railway authorities were not informed of the specific purpose of delivery of the sewing machine namely business during a festival.

16.4. Calculation of the Damage

In case of a contract for sale of good the damages are calculated on the basis of the difference between contract price and market price as on the date of breach.

For a breach by buyer,

Damages = Contract Price – Market Price

For a breach by seller,

Damages = Market Price – Contract Price

Where the seller retains the goods after the contract has been broken by the buyer, the seller cannot recover from the buyer any further loss even if the market falls. Again he is not liable to have the damages reduced if the market rises.

16.5. Duty to mitigate loss

Law casts a duty on the person who suffers losses on account of breach of contract by the other party must take all reasonable steps to mitigate the loss.

For example, if a buyer refuses to accept delivery and make payment of consignment of 100 bags of rice. The seller must try to find a new buyer and not let the stock perish from carelessness.

Compensation for Breach of Contract where the Penalty is stipulated for

At times, a contract may provide for a pre-estimate of compensation payable in case of its breach. The aim of such estimation is to avoid prolongation of dispute that may arise in future.

If the estimate is genuine compensation, it is called liquidated damages. If it is extravagant amount, it is termed as penalty.

The law states that in such cases, the party affected by the breach of contract is entitled to only to a reasonable compensation not exceeding the amount mentioned in the contract.

16.6. Other remedies for Breach

Apart from damages, the following remedies are also available to a Party affected by breach of contract -

(i) Rescission of contract

Where one party breaches the contract, the other party can treat it as rescinded. That is, the other party is absolved of his obligation to perform his part of the contract.

(ii) Suit upon quantum meruit

The phrase "quantum meruit" means "as much as earned". For example, A person begins a civil contract work. He has to stop the work later for some reason beyond his control. He is entitled to receive compensation on the principle of 'Quantum Meruit', that is, in proportion to the work done.

(iii) Suit for specific performance

At times, the nature of contract is such that the damages for its breach are not sufficient remedy. In such cases a party may seek specific performance of the contract. That is direct the party in breach, to carry out his promise according to the terms of the contract. This remedy is at the discretion of the court.

17. CONTINGENT CONTRACTS

A contingent contract is a contract to do or not do something, if some event, collateral to such contract, does or does not happen. Thus its essentials are -

(i) The agreement must be valid.

(ii) The performance is conditional.

(iii) Conditional on happening or not happening of an uncertain event.

(iv) The event must be collateral to the contract.

(v) The event must not be part of contract, that is, the event should be neither performance of promise nor a consideration for a promise.

For example, A promises to pay B Rs. One lakh, if B's house is destroyed by fire. This is a contingent contract.

But where A promises to deliver 100 bags of wheat and B agrees to pay after delivery. The contract is a conditional one and not a contingent contract.

17.1. Rules Relating to Enforcement

(a) Contract Contingent on "happening of an event"

Where a contingent contract is made contingent on happening of an event, it is enforced when the event happens. If the happening of event becomes impossible, the contract becomes void.

For example, A makes a contract with B to buy B's horse, if A survives C. This contract cannot be enforced by law unless and until C dies in A's lifetime.

(b) Contract Contingent non-happening of an event

Where a contingent contract is made contingent on a non-happening of an event, it can be enforced only when its happening becomes impossible.

For example, A agrees to pay B a sum of money if a certain ship does not return. The ship is sunk. The contract can be enforced when the ship sinks.

(c) Contract Contingent on the future conduct of a living person

If the future event on which a contract is contingent is the way in which a person will act at an unspecified time, the event shall be considered to become impossible when such person does anything which renders it impossible that he should so act within any definite time, or otherwise than under further contingencies.

For example, A agrees to pay B a sum of money if B marries C. C marries D. The marriage of B to C must now be considered impossible, although it is possible that D may die and that C may afterwards marry B.

(d) Agreement Contingent on an impossible event

A contingent agreement to do or not to do a thing if an impossible event happens is void. Such an agreement cannot be enforced. For example, A agrees to pay B a certain sum of money if Sun rises in the west next morning. This is an impossible event and hence void.

17.2. Contingent Contract and Wager

Although a contingent contract may appear similar to a wager, but there is a marked difference between the two. A wager is in form of a bet and parties have no other interest in the agreement. Whereas in a contingent contract parties have interest in the subject matter. The uncertain event must be collateral to the contract. A wagering agreement is void where as a contingent contract is valid.

18. QUASI CONTRACTS

There are situations where even in absence of contract, certain social relationships result in specific obligation towards specific person. They are not contracts because parties have no prior consensus. But the facts of the circumstances are such that a similar relation is presumed. These are known as quasi contracts.

Quasi contracts are based on principles of equity, justice and good conscience. They are based on the equitable principle that a person shall not be allowed to enrich himself at the expense of another. They are not from the agreement but are imposed by the law for an orderly and just society. These are neither torts as here the obligation is towards specific person.

Law enumerates following five circumstances as quasi-contracts -

18.1. Claim for necessaries supplied to persons incapable of contracting

When a person incapable of entering into contract, such as minor or lunatic, or his dependents are supplied with necessaries suited to his condition in life, the person supplying such necessaries is entitled to claim the price from the person's property.

For example, A supplies B, a lunatic or B's wife or child, with necessaries suitable to their condition in life. A is entitled to be reimbursed from B's property.

It is important that the supplies are limited to necessaries and no claim for luxury articles can be made.

18.2. Reimbursement of money paid due to another

A person who has paid a sum of money which another is obliged to pay, is entitled to be reimbursed by that other person provided the payment has been made by him to protect his own interest.

For example, B holds land in Bengal, on a lease granted by A, the zamindar. The revenue payable by A to the Government being in arrear, his land is advertised for sale by the Government. Under the revenue law, the consequence of such sale will be the annulment of B's lease. B, to prevent the sale and the consequent annulment of his own lease, pays to the Government the sum due from A. A is bound to make good to B the amount so paid.

18.3. Obligation of person enjoying benefits of non-gratuitous act

Where a person lawfully does or delivers anything to another, not intending to do so gratuitously, and such other person enjoys the benefit thereof, the latter is bound to restore the thing or make compensation to the former.

For example, A, a trader, leaves goods at B's house by mistake. B treats the goods as his own. He is bound to pay A for them.

18.4. Responsibility of finder of goods

A person who finds goods belonging to another and takes them into his custody, is subject to the same responsibility as a bailee. Thus, his duties are -

(i) Take proper care of the property as man of ordinary prudence would take.

(ii) Not to appropriate the goods.

(iii) Restore the goods to its owner, if the owner is found.

For example, A, a shop owner, finds a gold ear ring in his shop. He has CCTVs installed in his shop, but he does not care to examine the footage. Nor keep it in safe, as the item requires. But keeps it on his desk, from where it goes missing. A is liable to compensate the owner of the ear ring for the loss.

It is important to note that the finder of goods can claim reimbursement for expenditure incurred for preserving the goods and in searching the true owner. He may also claim any award, if announced by the owner. If the real owner refuses to pay the compensation or the award, the finder can exercise his right of lien, that is, refuse to deliver the article.

Finder of goods may also sell the goods under certain conditions.

(a) When a thing which is commonly the subject of sale is lost,

(b) If the owner cannot with reasonable diligence be found, or

(c) If he refuses, upon demand, to pay the lawful charges of the finder,

The finder may sell it -

(i) when the thing is in danger of perishing or of losing the greater part of its value, or,

(ii) when the lawful charges of the finder, in respect of the thing found, amount to two-thirds of its value.

18.5. Liability for money paid or thing delivered by mistake or by coercion

A person to whom money has been paid, or anything delivered, by mistake or under coercion, must repay or return it.

For example, A orders a pizza over a phone call. The delivery boy mistakenly delivers it to B. B eats the pizza. B is bound to pay the price of the pizza.

In all the above cases the contractual liability arises without any agreement between the parties.

LAW OF CRIMES

1. Introduction

The term "Crimes" has not been defined under any Indian enactment. Indian Penal Code, 1860 (or IPC) and Bharatiya Nyay Sanhita, 2023 (or BNS) define the term "offence" as a thing made punishable by IPC and Sanhita respectively. Although the term "Crime" is hard to define, generally it is used to denote a punishable wrong.

Blackstone has defined Crime as an act committed or omitted in violation of a public law either forbidding or commanding it.

Stephen says that A crime is a violation of a right considered in reference to the evil tendency of such violation as regards the community at large.

But, take for example, a company, whose management fail to manage its affairs properly. The factory is closed, workers are rendered unemployed, production of a commodity essential for the society is stopped. It is an act, which is injurious to public at large but can we prosecute the management for any crimes? The answer is most probably Not.

Given the difficulty, Crime may be understood from its components. Crime has following components -

(a) Act involving injury to People.

(b) State's desire to prevent such injury.

(c) Desire represented in form of threat of sanction or punishment.

(d) Legal proceedings aimed to conclude the question of guilt.

This, too, may appear technical. But one important thing to remember in respect of crimes is that nothing can be classified as a crime unless it has been so designated by any legislative enactment. Only if the law provides for trial of and punishment for a wrong, the act is termed as an offence. The Indian law of Crimes is contained in Indian Penal Code, 1860, the trial is conducted as per provisions of Code of Criminal Procedure, 1973 (Cr.P.C.) and the evidence is led and appreciated as per the provisions of Indian Evidence Act, 1872.

With the introduction of three New Criminal Laws, IPC, Cr.P.C. and Evidence Act have been replaced by Bharatiya Nyay Sanhita, 2023 (or BNS), Bharatiya Nagrik Suraksha Sanhita, 2023 (or BNSS) and Bharatiya Sakshya Adhiniyam, 2023 (or BSA) respectively.

2. ELEMENTS OF CRIME

The fundamental principal of criminal liability is that there must be a wrongful act – actus reus, combined with a wrongful intention, mens rea. This principle is embodied in the maxim – actus non facit reum nisi mens sit rea. It means an act does not make one guilty unless the mind is also guilty. Alternatively, a mere criminal intention not acted upon does not constitute a crime. There are four elements of a crime -

(i) Mens rea

(ii) Actus reus

(iii) Injury

(iv) Person

We shall discuss each of these elements in detail.

3. MENS REA

Mens rea is the mental element of Crime. The essence of criminal law is expressed in form of maxim - "actus non facit reum nisi mens sit rea" meaning an act does not make anyone guilty unless there is a criminal intent or a guilty mind. That is, for any act to be illegal in nature it must be done with a guilty mind. There can be no crime large or small, without an evil mind. The state of mind gives meaning to the act, and a crime is not committed unless there is intention to cause injury.

Mens rea is a legal phrase used to describe the mental state of a person, while doing any act. For example, in the case of murder, it is intention to cause death. In the case of theft, an intention is to steal. In the case of rape an intention to have forcible sexual connection with a woman without her consent, in the case of receiving stolen property, knowledge that the goods were stolen, and in the case of homicide by rash and negligent act, recklessness or negligence.

Mens rea is an age old concept. Even Indian criminal law has recognized the concept of mens rea, but in more specific and concrete manner rather than the original abstract form. Provisions of Penal Code (IPC and BNS) uses terms like intention, knowledge, and negligence. Further terms like voluntarily, wrongful gain, wrongful loss, dishonestly, fraudulently have been used. All these words represent the required state of the guilty mind or mens rea to be held guilty for an offence.

It is also worth noting, that IPC and BNS enumerate certain general exceptions. If a case is covered under general exceptions, the same cannot amount to an offence. Basically, these general exceptions denote circumstances under which the act is not accompanied with requisite mens rea.

Mens rea may take following forms -

3.1. Intention

Although the term 'Intention' has not been defined, but an act is said to be intended, when the consequence of an act are foreseen as well as desired. Law also uses term 'Voluntarily'. A person is said to cause an effect voluntarily when he causes it by means whereby he intended to cause it, or by means which at the time of employing those means he knows or had reason to believe to be likely to cause it.

Intention differs from motive. Motive is the ulterior design with which the act is committed while Intention is immediate. Motive may be good or bad, but it does not effect its illegality. Although good motive may be a mitigating factor in sentencing. Thus, a person committing theft of bread to feed his ailing child, is nonetheless guilty of theft, though his motive cannot be said to be improper in strict sense. Motive is not an element of crime.

3.2. Recklessness or Gross Negligence

Recklessness means that state of mind where the person does not desire the consequences but they are foreseeable to person of ordinary prudence and despite this forseability, the person disregard their seriousness or capacity to cause injury.

For example, A points a gun, not knowing whether it is loaded or not, on to B and presses the trigger. Here, A may desire that the gun is unloaded and does not fire. But he has foresight of the possible injury. His pressing the trigger amounts to acting in total disregard of the same.

Thus, recklessness is a state of mind in which a person does not care about the consequences of his or her actions.

3.3. Knowledge

Knowledge is also part of the mens rea whenever any person does any act having knowledge of its consequences then it is called as an intentional act. Knowledge is awareness on the part of the person concerned indicating his mind. A person can be supposed to know when there is a direct appeal to his sense knowledge is an awareness of the consequences of the act.

Knowledge is essentially subjective. In various cases intention and knowledge merge into each other and mean the same thing. More or less an intention can be presumed from the knowledge. Knowledge and intention have a very thin difference. Knowledge in contrast of intention, signifies a state of mental realization in which the mind is a passive recipient of certain ideas in it, while intention connotes a conscious state of mind in which mental faculties are summoned into action for the deliberate, prior conceived and perceived consequences.

3.4. Negligence

Negligence means neglect or failure to exercise reasonable and proper care that the circumstances require to guard against any injury to persons generally or to specific individual. A person is negligent when he fails to exercise due care and caution while doing any lawful act.

The concept of reasonable care is not define anywhere, however the test of the reasonable care is depend on the view of prudent man. While performing any act the person must take care as a prudent man takes, that is called a reasonable care. Any person, who fails to take requisite care and caution, and causes injury to any person, he is said to have done a negligent act.

Generally, mens rea for a crime must take form of intention, knowledge or recklessness, but at times it may also be in form of negligence. Negligence is indeed, almost aberrant ground for criminal liability. But the law may provide for punishment of negligent acts also.

Law may also provide for punishment of offence sans mens rea. They are called strict liability offence.

4. ACTUS REUS

Actus reus is the physical element of a Crime. It is something more than a mere thought or intention. An act is, defined as an event subject to the control of the will. In other words, an act means something voluntarily done by human being, An act consists of following three parts -

(i) Bodily activity or willed movement or omission.

(ii) Circumstances, in which it is done.

(iii) Consequences that arise from it.

For example, if A shoots B to death with a rifle, the mental element of act are first is origin or primary stage, namely a serious of muscular contractions by which the rifle is raised and the trigger is pulled. Secondly the circumstances, the fact that the rifle is loaded and is in working order, and that the person killed is within range. Thirdly the consequences, the fall of the trigger, explosion of the power, the discharge of the bullet, striking of the body of the victim, resulting in his death. All these facts are implied in the statement A killed B and they constitute an act for which he will be criminally liable.

4.1. Result of Conduct

To constitute a crime, there must always be result brought about by human conduct, a physical event which the law prohibits. Once the desired act is accomplished, the actus reus of crime is complete. How the contemplated event took place is not of much significance except for the purpose of fixing criminal liability. If the desired result is not achieved, the person is not responsible for the intended criminal act, which could not materialize. But if the act was sufficient in ordinary course to nature to bring about the intended result, which for some reason beyond the control of the person committing the act, he shall be liable for attempt.

4.2. Act or Omission prohibited by Law

To establish actus reus, it must be proved that the accused was responsible for a deed prohibited by criminal law. Only such acts that are prohibited or forbidden by law are crime. No crime is committed when a person exercises his lawful right, such as right of private defence. Similarly, omission is crime only when there is a legal duty to act. For example, if an onlooker who happens to be a good swimmer does not rescue a child about to be drowned in a pond he is not liable for any offence because there was no legal duty on his part to rescue a person. But where a parent omits to feed an infant, or provides necessary care, the same may amount to an offence.

5. PERSON

Person means entity recognised by law as capable of owning rights and being subject of duties. In order to constitute a crime, it is important for somebody to commit it. The law should always be able to pinpoint the person who is responsible for committing an offence. The term "person" is not limted only to a human being. It also includes legal persons such as a company and an association or body of persons.

6. INJURY

The last of the basic elements of crime is injury. There can be no crime if no person faces some kind of an injury. Injury means any harm caused to a person illegally either in mind, body, reputation or property. However, there can be some crimes which might not require injury to any person. For example, driving without a driving license is a crime even if it may not harm anybody.

7. GENERAL DEFINITIONS

Law provides for definitions of certain words that are used repeatedly in the Penal Code. The purpose is to give them a definite meaning and avoid repetition. We shall have a look at some of the most important terms of the IPC / BNS.

1. Wrongful gain

Wrongful Gain means gain of property by unlawful means to which the person gaining is not legally entitled.

2. Wrongful loss

Wrongful Loss means loss of property by unlawful means to which the person losing it is legally entitled.

3. Gaining wrongfully.

A person is said to gain wrongfully when such person retains wrongfully, as well as when such person acquires wrongfully.

4. Losing wrongfully.

A person is said to lose wrongfully when such person is wrongfully kept out of any property, as well as when such person is wrongfully deprived of property.

4. Dishonestly

Whoever does anything with the intention of <u>causing wrongful gain to one person or wrongful loss to another person,</u> is said to do that thing "dishonestly".

5. Fraudulently

A person is said to do a thing fraudulently if he does that thing with <u>intent to defraud</u> but not otherwise.

6. Reason to believe

A person is said to have "reason to believe" a thing, if he has <u>sufficient cause to believe</u> that thing but not otherwise.

7. Document

Document denotes any matter expressed or described upon any substance, by means of letters, figures or marks, or by more than one of those means and intended to be used, or which may be used, as evidence of that matter

Explanation 1.--It is immaterial by what means or upon what substance the letters, figures or marks are formed, or whether the evidence is intended for, or may be used in, a Court of Justice, or not.

Illustrations

(i) A writing expressing the terms of a contract, which may be used as evidence of the contract, is a document.

(ii) A cheque upon a banker is a document.

(iii) A power-of-attorney is a document.

(iv) A map or plan which is intended to be used or which may be used as evidence, is a document.

(v) A writing containing directions or instructions is a document.

Explanation 2.--Whatever is expressed by means of letters, figures or marks as explained by mercantile or other usage, shall be deemed to be expressed by such letters, figures or marks within the meaning of this section, although the same may not be actually expressed.

Illustration

(i) A writes his name on the back of a bill of exchange payable to his order. The meaning of the endorsement as explained by mercantile usage, is that the bill is to be paid to the holder. The endorsement is a document, and must be construed in the same manner as if the words "pay to the holder" or words to that effect had been written over the signature.

8. Valuable security

Valuable Security denotes a document which is, or purports to be, a document whereby any legal right is created, extended, transferred, restricted, extinguished or released, or whereby any person acknowledges that he lies under legal liability, or has not a certain legal right.

Illustration

(i) A writes his name on the back of a bill of exchange. As the effect of this endorsement is to transfer the right to the bill to any person who may become the lawful holder of it, the endorsement is a "valuable security".

9. Act

The word "act" denotes as well as series of acts as a single act

10. Omission

The word "omission" denotes as well a series of omissions as a single omission.

11. Voluntarily

A person is said to cause an effect "voluntarily" when he causes it by means whereby he intended to cause it, or by means which, at the time of employing those means, he knew or had reason to believe to be likely to cause it.

Illustration

(i) A sets fire, by night, to an inhabited house in a large town, for the purpose of facilitating a robbery and thus causes the death of a person. Here, A may not have intended to cause death; and may even be sorry that death has been caused by his act; yet, if he knew that he was likely to cause death, he has caused death voluntarily.

12. Illegal

Everything which is an offence or prohibited by law, or furnishes ground for a Civil Action.

13. Injury

Any harm illegally caused to any person in Body, Mind, Reputation or Property.

14. Good faith

Nothing is said to be done or believed in "good faith" which is done or believed without due care and attention.

8. GENERAL EXCEPTIONS

Similar to tort, law recognises certain exceptional conditions in which the act that appears to satisfy the definition prescribed for the offence, nonetheless lacks in certain aspect (generally mens rea or the guilty mind) for it to be punished. The law provides that every definition of an offence, every penal provision and every illustration of every such definition or penal provision shall be understood subject to these exceptions. Again the idea is to provide lucidity to the large text and avoid repetition. The importance of these exceptions is that once a case falls into an exception, the same does not amount to an offence. The general exceptions are as follows -

8.1. Mistake of Fact

The law states that when a person is bound by law to perform any act, his act shall not amount to an offence. It is quite basic that when on one hand the law compels performance, it cannot on the other prohibit it at the same time. This defence is also available where a person by reason of a mistake of fact, and not by reason of mistake of law, in good faith believes himself to be bound by law to do it. That is, the law gives due regard to a bona fide mistake of fact, but not of law. The essential of this exception are -

(a) Act is done by a person who is bound by law, or

(b) Who by reason of a mistake of fact in good faith believes himself to be so bound,

(c) But not by reason of a mistake of law.

Illustrations

(i) A, a soldier, fires on a mob by the order of his superior officer, in conformity with the commands of the law. A has committed no offence.

(ii) A, an officer of a Court of Justice, being ordered by that Court to arrest Y, and after due enquiry, believing Z to be Y, arrests Z. A has committed no offence.

Similarly, if a person is justified by law, or by reason of a mistake of fact and not by reason of a mistake of law in good faith, believes himself to be justified by law, in doing an act, the same is not an offence.

Illustration

(i) A sees Z commit what appears to A to be a murder. A, in the exercise, to the best of his judgment exerted in good faith, of the power which the law gives to all persons of apprehending murderers in the fact, seizes Z, in order to bring Z before the proper authorities. A has committed no offence, though it may turn out that Z was acting in self-defence.

8.2. Judicial Acts

Law gives protection to actions of Judges exercising their judicial powers accorded by the law. The exception also extends to other persons who execute such judicial orders, say warrant of arrest. The scope of exception is not only the exercise of a vested judicial power but also exercise of such power which the Judge believed in good faith to be given to him by law. Thus, law provides for protection to judicial acts and also errors made in good faith.

8.3. Accident

Act of misfortune or accident are no offence. Though some person may be instrumental in the occurrence of an accident, but if he has acted without any criminal intention or knowledge and does any lawful act in a lawful manner by lawful means and also employs proper care and caution, he cannot be held liable under criminal law for the consequence incurred. Thus, ingredients of this exception are -

(a) Act is result of accident or misfortune,

(b) Act is done without any criminal intention or knowledge,

(c) Act is lawful,

(d) Act is done in a lawful manner by lawful means,

(e) Act is done with proper care and caution.

It can be understood that if the above conditions are satisfied, the act cannot be said to have accompanied with mens rea.

Illustration

(i) A is at work with a hatchet; the head flies off and kills a man who is standing by. Here, if there was no want of proper caution on the part of A, his act is excusable and not an offence.

8.4. Act of Necessity

Necessity knows no law. At times, a person may be induced to perform certain detrimental act in order to prevent or avoid bigger harm to person or property. Law provides that if such acts of necessity are done without any criminal intention and in good faith, the same is no offence. Thus, ingredients of this exception are -

(a) Act is done with the knowledge that it is likely to cause harm,

(b) But act is done without any criminal intention to cause harm,

(c) For the purpose of preventing or avoiding other harm to person or property,

(d) In Good faith

Illustration

(i) A, the captain of a steam vessel, suddenly, and without any fault or negligence on his part, finds himself in such a position that, before he can stop his vessel, he must inevitably run down a boat B, with twenty or thirty passengers on board, unless he changes the course of his vessel, and that, by changing his course, he must incur risk of running down a boat C with only two passengers on board, which he may possibly clear. Here, if A alters his course without any intention to run down the boat C and in good faith for the purpose of avoiding the danger to the passengers in the boat B, he is not guilty of an offence, though he may run down the boat C by doing an act which he knew was likely to cause that effect, if it be found as a matter of fact that the danger which he intended to avoid was such as to excuse him in incurring the risk of running down C.

8.5. Doli Incapex

The term "doli incapex" means incapable of committing a crime. The law provides complete immunity to a child below seven years of age. The law presumes that a child below such age does not have sufficient maturity to understand the nature and consequences of his actions.

For a child between seven and twelve years of age, law provides for conditional immunity. Such a child, who has not attained sufficient maturity of understanding to judge the nature and consequences of his conduct on that occasion, is also covered under the exception.

8.6. Unsound Mind

The term "unsound mind" is not defined under the law, but it refers to various forms of insanity. The law does not absolve all persons suffering from any kind of mental ailment. But the test is whether the person was, at the time of doing it, by reason of unsoundness of mind, incapable of knowing the nature of the act, or that he is doing what is either wrong or contrary to law. That is, to avail this defence, following must be established -

(a) Act is done by a person of unsound mind,

(b) He is unsound at the time of doing it,

(c) Incapable of knowing the nature of the act, or

(d) What is either wrong or contrary to law

Only if the above conditions are satisfied, the person may claim the benefit.

8.7. Intoxication

Involuntary intoxication has been recognised as a defence. The law states that nothing is an offence which is done by a person who, at the time of doing it, is, by reason of intoxication, incapable of knowing the nature of the act, or that he is doing what is either wrong, or contrary to law; provided that the thing which intoxicated him was administered to him without his knowledge or against his will.

Thus, the first and foremost condition for defence of intoxication is that it should not be voluntary. Intoxication should have been without knowledge or against will, and the level of intoxication must be such that rendered the person incapable of knowing the nature of the act, or what is either wrong, or contrary to law.

8.8. Consent

Although crime is an act against society, consent of the intended victim is still a good defence. The defence of Consent basically has three forms. Firstly, it can be given by an adult individual to suffer harm irrespective of benefit. Secondly, it can be given to obtain certain benefit. Thirdly, it can be given by guardian for benefit of a child.

(i) Personal Consent

Man is risk taking and adventure seeking by nature. He has gained a lot by them too. Tiresome sea voyages and finding new lands is prime example of the same. Ancient and Modern day sports have risk elements built in. The law provides that an adult person of sound mind may give consent to suffer risk of harm. The act may or may not be for any intended benefit. But there is a limit to the risk to which a person may consent, that is the act must not be intended or likely to cause death or grievous hurt. Thus, essentials of this defence are -

(a) Act is not intended or likely to cause death, or grievous hurt.

(b) Person consents to suffer harm.

(c) Consent may be express or implied.

(d) Person giving consent must be above eighteen years of age.

Illustration

(i) A and Z agree to fence with each other for amusement. This agreement implies the consent of each to suffer any harm which, in the course of such fencing, may be caused without foul play; and if A, while playing fairly, hurts Z, A commits no offence.

(ii) For Beneficial Act

At times, a beneficial act may have an element of risk. But the possible benefit outweighs the risk involved. Surgical treatment is a simple example of the situation, where there is instantaneous bodily harm for a healthy life in longer run. In such cases too, a person may consent to risk of harm. The essential ingredients of this defence are -

(i) Act is not intended to cause death,

(ii) Act is for benefit of the person,

(iii) Person has given his consent to suffer that harm, or to take the risk of that harm,

(iv) Consent may be express or implied,

(v) Act done in Good Faith

Illustration

(i) A, a surgeon, knowing that a particular operation is likely to cause the death of Z, who suffers under the painful complaint, but not intending to cause Z's death, and intending, in good faith, Z's benefit, performs that operation on Z, with Z's consent. A has committed no offence.

(iii) Benefit of Child

Similarly, a benefit for child or unsound may involve some form of harm. In such cases too, the guardian may himself perform the beneficial act or give consent for the same. Essential conditions are as follows -

(a) Act is done in good faith,

(b) For the benefit of a person,

(c) Person is under twelve years of age, or of unsound mind,

(d) Act is done by or by consent of the guardian or other person having lawful charge of that person,

(e) Consent may be express or implied

This exception is not applicable to -

(a) Intentional causing of death, or its attempt;

(b) Act likely to cause death, for any purpose other than the preventing of death or grievous hurt, or the curing of any grievous disease or infirmity;

(c) Voluntary causing of grievous hurt, or its attempt, unless it be for the purpose of preventing death or grievous hurt, or the curing of any grievous disease or infirmity;

(d) Abetment of any offence, to the committing of which offence it would not extend.

Illustration

(i) A, in good faith, for his child's benefit without his child's consent, has his child cut for the stone by a surgeon knowing it to be likely that the operation will cause the child's death, but not intending to cause the child's death. A is within the exception, in as much as his object was the cure of the child.

What is not a valid Consent?

A valid consent must be free will of a competent mind. Thus, a consent given under following cases is invalid -

(a) Fear of injury

(b) Misconception of fact

(c) By insane person

(d) By person of unsound mind

(e) By intoxicated person

(f) By Child under twelve years of age.

When consent inapplicable?

The defence of consent is inapplicable to acts which are offences independently of any harm they may cause.

Illustration

(i) Causing miscarriage (unless caused in good faith for the purpose of saving the life of the woman) is offence independently of any harm which it may cause or be intended to cause to the woman. Therefore, it is not an offence "by reason of such harm"; and the consent of the woman or of her guardian to the causing of such miscarriage does not justify the act.

8.9. Beneficial Act without Consent

Situation may arise where beneficial act must be performed in the larger interest of a person, but such person is unable to give valid consent, nor any other person is available to give consent on his behalf. Thus, its essentials are -

(a) Act is for benefit of Person,

(b) Act is done Without Person's consent,

(c) Circumstances are such that it is impossible for that person to signify consent, or if that person is incapable of giving consent, has no guardian or other person in lawful charge of him from whom it is possible to obtain consent in time,

(d) Act is done in Good Faith.

This exception is not applicable to -

(a) Intentional causing of death, or its attempt;

(b) Act likely to cause death, for any purpose other than the preventing of death or grievous hurt, or the curing of any grievous disease or infirmity;

(c) Voluntary causing of hurt, or its attempt, for any purpose other than preventing of death or hurt;

(d) Abetment of any offence, to the committing of which offence it would not extend.

Illustrations

(i) Z is thrown from his horse, and is insensible. A, a surgeon, finds that Z requires to be trepanned. A, not intending Z's death, but in good faith, for Z's benefit, performs the trepan before Z recovers his power of judging for himself. A has committed no offence.

(ii) Z is carried off by a tiger. A fires at the tiger knowing it to be likely that the shot may kill Z, but not intending to kill Z, and in good faith intending Z's benefit. A's ball gives Z a mortal wound. A has committed no offence.

8.10. Communication in Good Faith

No communication made in good faith is an offence by reason of any harm to the person to whom it is made, if it is made for the benefit of that person. That is -

(a) Communication is made to a person,

(b) Communication is for the benefit of that person,

(c) Communication is made in good faith.

Illustration

(i) A, a surgeon, in good faith, communicates to a patient his opinion that he cannot live. The patient dies in consequence of the shock. A has committed no offence, though he knew it to be likely that the communication might cause the patient's death.

8.11. Actions compelled by Threat

The evil in man can sometimes take form of threat. That is, a person may not perform wrongful act himself, but compel other to do so. In such cases, the person acting lacks required mens rea and law provides exception for him. The essential ingredients for this defence are -

(a) Person is compelled to do the act by threats,

(b) Threat is made at the time of doing the act,

(c) Threat gives reasonable apprehension of instant death,

(d) Person has not placed himself in such constraint,

(e) Defence is not available to offence of murder and offences against the State punishable with death.

8.12. Trifle Act

Where an act causes or intended to cause or known to be likely to cause any harm, which is so slight that no person of ordinary sense and temper would complain of such harm, the act is covered under the general exception of trifle act. The same amounts to no offence.

8.13. Private Defence

Every person has right to defend his life and property against unlawful aggression. Every person has a right, to defend -

(a) His own body, and the body of any other person, against any offence affecting the human body;

(b) Any movable or immovable property, of himself or of any other person, against offence of -

(i) Theft,

(ii) Robbery,

(iii) Mischief,

(iv) Criminal trespass,

(v) Attempt of any of the above

The right of private defence is quite elaborate and even extends to causing death of aggressor in certain circumstances. Right of private defence of body extends to causing death of the assailant, where the assault is with intention of or reasonably cause apprehension of -

(a) Death,

(b) Grievous hurt,

(c) Rape,

(d) Gratifying unnatural lust,

(e) Kidnapping or abduction,

(f) Wrongfully confinement where there is apprehension that he will be unable to have recourse to the public authorities for his release,

(g) Act of throwing or administering acid with apprehension of grievous hurt.

Right of private defence of property extends to causing death of the assailant, against the following offences -

(a) Robbery,

(b) House-breaking by night,

(c) Mischief by fire committed on any building, tent or vessel, which building, tent or vessel is used as a human dwelling, or as a place for the custody of property,

(d) Theft, mischief, or house-trespass, with reasonable apprehension of death or grievous hurt.

But the right of defence is limited to exercise of defence. It cannot take form of offence or aggression. Thus, the right begins with the threat and continues till the threat continues. Once the threat comes to an end, so does the right. Further, the harm that may be inflicted as defence, must be proportional to the threat.

Illustration

(i) A, a gunda, assaults B by pointing a knife at him. B takes out a pistol. B commits no offence by showing the gun, though he has a definite advantage over knife. But B may not shoot A, unless the threat is in nature of immediate death or grievous hurt. Further, if A is alarmed and effects retreat, the right of private defence comes to an end.

9. LIABILITY FOR ACTS OF OTHERS

The IPC and BNS contain several provisions imposing criminal liability for wrongful acts committed by others. They are based on the principal that although one person may seem to perform the wrongful act, but in reality he does it at behest of other or others. In such circumstances, that other must not be absolved of his liability merely because he did not pull the trigger himself. Instances of such liability may be categorised as follows -

1. Common Intention,

2. Common Object of Unlawful Assembly,

3. Abetment,

4. Criminal Conspiracy.

9.1. Common Intention

Penal Code provides that when an act done by several persons in furtherance of common intention of all, each of such persons is liable for that act in the same manner as if it is done by him alone. The requirements for application of this principal are as follows -

(a) A criminal act,

(b) Act is done by several persons,

(c) Active participation of all the persons,

(d) In furtherance of common intention of all,

(e) Prior meeting of minds.

When the criminal act complained against is done by one of the accused persons in the furtherance of the common intention of all, then liability for the crime may be imposed on any one of the persons in the same manner as if the act were done by him alone.

The rule is particularly important in cases where the acts of individual perpetrators cannot be distinguished from one another or that each played a part which was incomplete in itself. For example, where two persons tie a rope around the neck of another and each pulls one end of the rope. Both can say that neither was alone capable of causing death of the victim. But the principal of common intention will deny them such an absurd defence plea.

Also, one must not confuse common intention with similar or same intention. Two persons may have same intention without having knowledge of the intention of the other. They may also know each other's intention but may act independently of one other. In such cases, they have similar intention but not common intention. In such cases, each is liable for his act alone and not of the other.

The most important aspect of common intention is prior meeting of minds. This prior meeting need not be a prior physical meeting. It may even develop in spur of a moment, but it must be shared or conveyed among one another.

9.2. Common Object of Unlawful Assembly

Penal Code provides that if an offence is committed by any member of an unlawful assembly in prosecution of the common object of that assembly, every person who at the time of committing of that offence is the member of the same assembly is guilty of that offence. The requirements for application of this principal are as follows -

(a) An unlawful assembly,

(b) Criminal act is committed by any member or members of such assembly,

(c) Act done is for prosecution of the common object of the assembly or it was likely to be committed in prosecution of the common object,

(d) Members must have voluntarily joined the unlawful assembly,

(e) Member had knowledge of the common object of the assembly,

(f) Mere presence of the member is sufficient to be held liable, there need not be any active participation on his part.

An unlawful assembly is an assembly of five or more persons whose common object is to -

(a) Overawe by criminal force or assault any government or public servant in the exercise of the lawful power,

(b) Resist the execution of any law or legal process,

(c) Commit any mischief or criminal trespass, or other offence,

(d) Take or obtain possession of any property, or to deprive any person of a right or to enforce any right or supposed right by means of criminal force or assault,

(e) Compel any person to do what he is not legally bound to do, or to omit to do what he is legally entitled to do by means of criminal force or assault.

The rule of common object requires merely that the offence is committed by any member of an unlawful assembly in prosecution of its common object. Once the offence is committed, all members having voluntarily joined the assembly and having knowledge of the common object are liable. There may not be any active role. Merely becoming the member is sufficient actus reus in such cases. Again, the person may not have intended the act or may even be against it, but if he had knowledge or the offence was likely, the same is sufficient mens rea on his part.

9.3. Abetment

Abetment literally means to urge, induce or encourage. Penal Code does not define abetment, but merely prescribes modes in which one person may abet another to commit any offence. They are as follows -

(i) Abetment by Instigation,

(ii) Abetment by Conspiracy,

(iii) Intentional Aiding.

Instigation means to incite or provoke. Abetment by Instigation means when one person instigates other to commit any offence. Instigation may take any form. It may even be persuasion or mere approval. There can be instigation even by lying aimed to achieve desired result.

Illustration

(i) A, a public officer, is authorised by a warrant from a Court of Justice to apprehend Z, B, knowing that fact and also that C is not Z, wilfully represents to A that C is Z, and thereby intentionally causes A to apprehend C. Here B abets by instigation the apprehension of C.

Abetment by Conspiracy means to engage one or more persons to commit an offence. It is necessary some act or illegal omission must take place as a result of such conspiracy. Mere agreement is not sufficient to be held liable.

Intentionally aiding means directly assisting the commission of the offence, or facilitating the commission of the offence or omit what one is bound to do.

There are certain important rules pertaining to abetment. They help us to understand its scope better. They are -

(a) The abetment of illegal omission is an offence, although the abettor may not himself be bound to do that act.

(b) Abetted act need not be committed.

(c) Person Abetted need not be capable of committing an offence.

(d) The abetment of abetment of an offence is also an offence.

(e) Abettor need not Concert in the Abetment by Conspiracy

Illustrations

(i) A instigates B to murder C. B refuses to do so. A is guilty of abetting B to commit murder.

(ii) A instigates B to murder D. B in pursuance of the instigation stabs D. D recovers from the wound. A is guilty of instigating B to commit murder.

(iii) A, with a guilty intention, abets a child or a lunatic to commit an act which would be an offence, if committed by a person capable by law of committing an offence, and having the same intention as A. Here, whether the act be committed or not, A is guilty of abetting the offence.

(iv) A, intending to cause a theft to be committed, instigates B to take property belonging to Z out of Z's possession. A induces B to believe that the property belongs to A. B takes the property out of Z's possession, in good faith, believing it to be A's property. B, acting under this misconception, does not take dishonestly, and therefore does not commit theft. But A is guilty of abetting theft, and is liable to the same punishment as if B had committed theft.

(v) A instigates B to instigate C to murder Z. B accordingly instigates C to murder Z, and C commits that offence in consequence of B's instigation. A is also liable.

(vi) A concerts with B a plan for poisoning Z. It is agreed that A shall administer the poison. B then explains the plan to C mentioning that a third person is to administer the poison, but without mentioning A's name. C agrees to procure the poison, and procures and delivers it to B for the purpose of its being used in the manner explained. A administers the poison; Z dies in consequence. Here, though A and C have not conspired together, yet C has been engaged in the conspiracy in pursuance of which Z has been murdered. C has therefore committed the offence defined in this section and is liable to the punishment for murder.

9.4. Criminal Conspiracy

When two or more persons agree to do, or cause to be done an illegal act, or an act which is not illegal by illegal means, such an agreement is designated a criminal conspiracy. An agreement to commit an offence is itself Conspiracy. But in other cases, some act besides the agreement must be done by one or more parties in pursuance thereof.

The meeting of minds of two or more persons for doing an illegal act or an act by illegal means is a *sine qua non* of the criminal conspiracy. It is not necessary that every conspirator should take active part in commission of each and every part of conspiracy. They may have specific roles assigned to them, but they are constructively liable for the sum total of acts of all committed in pursuance of the conspiracy.

10. CLASSIFICATION OF OFFENCES

IPC, for the purpose of lucidity, classifies offences into various Chapters. Some of these chapters are further divided into several Headings. These chapters and headings have sections that spell out the definition and punishment of the various offences.

A brief description of Chapters and Headings is as follows -

Chapter VI - Offences Against State

121. Waging, or attempting to wage war, or abetting waging of war, against the Government of India.

124A. Sedition.

Chapter VII - Offences Relating to the Army, Navy and Air Force

131. Abetting mutiny, or attempting to seduce a soldier, sailor or airman from his duty.

135. Abetment of desertion of soldier, sailor or airman.

136. Harbouring deserter.

Chapter VIII - Offences against Public Tranquility

141. Unlawful assembly.

146. Rioting.

147. Punishment for rioting.

153A. Promoting enmity between different groups on grounds of religion, race, place of birth, residence. language, etc., and doing acts prejudicial to maintenance of harmony.

159. Affray.

160. Punishment for committing affray.

Chapter IX - Offences by or relating to Public Servants

166. Public servant disobeying law, with intent to cause injury to any person.

Chapter IX-A - Offences relating to Elections

Chapter X - Contempt of Lawful Authority of Public Servants

174. Non-attendance in obedience to an order from public servant.

174A. Non-appearance in response to a proclamation under section 82 of Act 2 of 1974.

177. Furnishing false information.

188. Disobedience to order duly promulgated by public servant.

189. Threat of injury to public servant.

Chapter XI - False Evidence and Offences against Public Justice

191. Giving false evidence.

192. Fabricating false evidence.

193. Punishment for false evidence.

201. Causing disappearance of evidence of offence, or giving false information, to screen offender

212. Harbouring offender.

Chapter XII - Offences relating to Coin and Government Stamps

231. Counterfeiting coin.

232. Counterfeiting Indian coin.

Chapter XIII - Offences relating to Weights and Measures

Chapter XIV - Offences Affecting Public Health, Safety, Convenience, Decency and Morals

268. Public nuisance.

269. Negligent act likely to spread infection of disease dangerous to life.

270. Malignant act likely to spread infection of disease dangerous to life.

271. Disobedience to quarantine rule.

272. Adulteration of food or drink intended for sale.

290. Punishment for public nuisance in cases not otherwise provided for.

294. Obscene acts and songs.

Chapter XV - Offences relating to Religion

295A. Deliberate and malicious acts, intended to outrage religious feelings of any class by insulting its religion or religious beliefs.

Chapter XVI - Offences affecting the Human Body

Offences affecting Life

299. Culpable homicide.

300. Murder. When culpable homicide is not murder.

302. Punishment for murder.

304. Punishment for culpable homicide not amounting to murder.

304A. Causing death by negligence.

354A. Sexual harassment and punishment for sexual harassment.

354B. Assault or use of criminal force to woman with intent to disrobe.

354C. Voyeurism.

354D. Stalking.

Kidnapping, Abduction, Slavery and Forced Labour

359. Kidnapping.

360. Kidnapping from India.

361. Kidnapping from lawful guardianship.

362. Abduction.

363. Punishment for kidnapping.

363A. Kidnapping or maiming a minor for purposes of begging.

366. Kidnapping, abducting or inducing woman to compel her marriage, etc.

Sexual Offences

375. Rape.

376. Punishment for rape.

Unnatural Offences

377. Unnatural offences.

Chapter XVII - Offences against Property
Theft

378. Theft.

379. Punishment for theft.

380. Theft in dwelling house, etc.

Extortion

383 Extortion.

384. Punishment for extortion.

386. Extortion by putting a person in fear of death on grievous hurt.

Robbery and Dacoity

390. Robbery. When theft is robbery. When extortion is robbery.

391. Dacoity.

392. Punishment for robbery.

395. Punishment for dacoity.

396. Dacoity with murder.

400. Punishment for belonging to gang of dacoits.

401. Punishment for belonging to gang of thieves.

Criminal Misappropriation of Property

403. Dishonest misappropriation of property.

404. Dishonest misappropriation of property possessed by deceased person at the time of his death.

Criminal Breach of Trust

405. Criminal breach of trust.

406. Punishment for criminal breach of trust.

409. Criminal breach of trust by public, servant. or by banker, merchant or agent.

Receiving of Stolen Property

410. Stolen property.

411. Dishonestly receiving stolen property.

413. Habitually dealing in stolen property.

Cheating

415. Cheating.

416. Cheating by personation.

417. Punishment for cheating.

419. Punishment for cheating by personation.

420. Cheating and dishonestly inducing delivery of property.

Fraudulent Deeds and Dispositions of Property

421. Dishonest or fraudulent removal or concealment of property to prevent distribution among creditor.

Mischief

425. Mischief.

426. Punishment for mischief.

436. Mischief by fire or explosive substance with intent to destroy house, etc.

Criminal Trespass

441. Criminal trespass.

442. House-trespass.

443. Lurking house-trespass.

445. House-breaking.

447. Punishment for criminal trespass.

448. Punishment for house-trespass.

451. House-trespass in order to commit offence punishable with imprisonment.

452. House-trespass after preparation for hurt, assault or wrongful restraint.

453. Punishment for lurking house-trespass or house-breaking.

457. Lurking house-trespass or house-breaking by night in order to commit offence punishable with imprisonment.

Chapter XVIII - Offences relating to Documents and Property Marks

463. Forgery.

464. Making a false document.

465. Punishment for forgery.

467. Forgery of valuable security, will, etc.

468. Forgery for purpose of cheating.

471. Using as genuine a forged document or electronic record.

Property and Other Marks

479. Property mark.

Using a false property mark.

Punishment for using a false property mark.

Currency-Notes and Bank-Notes

489A. Counterfeiting currency-notes or bank-notes.

489B. Using as genuine, forged or counterfeit currency-notes or bank-notes.

489C. Possession of forged or counterfeit currency notes or bank-notes.

Chapter XIX - Criminal Breach of Contracts of Service

491. Breach of contract to attend on and supply wants of helpless person.

Chapter XX - Offences relating to Marriage

493. Cohabitation caused by a man deceitfully inducing a belief of lawful marriage.

494. Marrying again during life-time of husband or wife.

495. Same offence with concealment of former marriage from person with whom subsequent marriage is contracted.

Bharatiya Nyay Sanhita, 2023 (BNS) has followed IPC to a large extent in terms of classification of offences into various Chapters. Similarly, some are further divided into Headings. These chapters and headings have sections that spell out the definition and punishment of the various offences.

A brief description of Chapters, Headings and Sections of BNS is as follows -

Chapter V – Offences against Woman and Children

Sexual offences
63. Rape.
64. Punishment for rape.
69. Sexual intercourse by employing deceitful means etc.
70. Gang rape.

Criminal force and assault against women
74. Assault or criminal force to woman with intent to outrage her modesty.
75. Sexual harassment and punishment for sexual harassment.
76. Assault or use of criminal force to woman with intent to disrobe.
77. Voyeurism.
78. Stalking.
79. Word, gesture or act intended to insult the modesty of a woman.

Offences relating to marriage
80. Dowry death.
82. Marrying again during lifetime of husband or wife.
84. Enticing or taking away or detaining with criminal intent a married woman.
85. Husband or relative of husband of a woman subjecting her to cruelty.
86. Cruelty defined.

Causing of Miscarriage, etc.
88. Causing miscarriage.
89. Causing miscarriage without woman's consent.

Offences against children
93. Exposure and abandonment of child under twelve years, by parent or person having care of it.
94. Concealment of birth by secret disposal of dead body.
95. Hiring, employing or engaging a child to commit an offence.
96. Procuration of child.

Chapter VI – Offences affecting Human Body

Offences affecting life
100. Culpable homicide.
101. Murder.

102. Culpable homicide by causing death of person other than person whose death was intended.

103. Punishment for murder.

104. Punishment for murder by life-convict.

105. Punishment for culpable homicide not amounting to murder.

106. Causing death by negligence.

107. Abetment of suicide of child or person with mental illness.

108. Abetment of suicide.

109. Attempt to murder.

110. Attempt to commit culpable homicide.

111. Organised crime.

112. Petty organised crime or organised in general.

113. Terrorist act.

Hurt

114. Hurt.

115. Voluntarily causing hurt.

116. Grievous hurt.

117. Voluntarily causing grievous hurt.

118. Voluntarily causing hurt or grievous hurt by dangerous weapons or means.

121. Voluntarily causing hurt or grievous hurt to deter public servant from his duty.

122. Voluntarily causing hurt or grievous hurt on provocation.

123. Causing hurt by means of poison, etc., with intent to commit an offence.

124. Voluntarily causing grievous hurt by use of acid, etc.

126. Wrongful restraint.

127. Wrongful confinement.

Criminal Force and Assault

128. Force.

129. Criminal force.

130. Assault.

131. Punishment for assault or criminal force otherwise than on grave provocation.

132. Assault or criminal force to deter public servant from discharge of his duty.

134. Assault or criminal force in attempt to commit theft of property carried by a person.

Kidnapping, Abduction, Slavery and Forced Labour

137. Kidnapping.

138. Abduction.

140. Kidnapping or abducting in order to murder or for ransom etc.

143. Habitual dealing in slaves.

144. Unlawful compulsory labour.

Chapter VII – Offences Against The State

147. Waging, or attempting to wage war, or abetting waging of war, against the Government of India.

152. Acts endangering sovereignty unity and integrity of India.

Chapter VIII – Offences relating to Army, Navy and Air Force

159. Abetting mutiny, or attempting to seduce a soldier, sailor or airman from his duty.

160. Abetment of mutiny, if mutiny is committed in consequence thereof.

Chapter IX – Offences relating to Elections

Chapter X – Offences relating to Coin, Currency-Notes, Bank-Notes and Government Stamps

Chapter XI – Offences against Public Tranquility

189. Unlawful assembly.

190. Every member of unlawful assembly guilty of offence committed in prosecution of common object.

191. Rioting.

194. Affray.

Chapter XII – Offences relating to Public Servants

198. Public servant disobeying law, with intent to cause injury to any person.

199. Public servant disobeying direction under law.

200. Punishment for non-treatment of victim.

Chapter XIII – Contempt Of Lawful Authority of Public Servants

206. Absconding to avoid service of summons or other proceeding.

207. Preventing service of summons or other proceeding, or preventing publication thereof.

208. Non-attendance in obedience to an order from public servant.

209. Non-appearance in response to a proclamation under section 84 of BNSS, 2023.

221. Obstructing public servant in discharge of public functions.

222. Omission to assist public servant when bound by law to give assistance.

223. Disobedience to order duly promulgated by public servant.

224. Threat of injury to public servant.

225. Attempt to commit suicide to compel or restraint exercise of lawful power.

Chapter XIV - False Evidence and Offences Against Public Justice

227. Giving false evidence

228. Fabricating false evidence

229. Punishment for false evidence

232. Threatening any person to give false evidence

249. Harbouring offender

355. Misconduct in public by a drunken person
356. Defamation
357. Breach of contract to attend on and supply wants of helpless person

The above list comprises of some of the important sections and offences. To discuss all would be to burden the reader with too much of the information. So, we shall discuss only a few most common offences.

11. CULPABLE HOMICIDE AND MURDER

Homicide means killing of a Human being by another human being. It can be justifiable (for example, killing of an enemy soldier in a war), culpable (that is blameworthy or wrongful) or accidental.

Culpable Homicide means causing death by -

(i) An act with the intention of causing death;

(ii) An act with the intention of causing such bodily injury as is likely to cause death; or

(iii) An act with the knowledge that it was likely to cause death.

Illustration

(i) A lays sticks and turf over a pit, with the intention of thereby causing death, or with the knowledge that death is likely to be thereby caused. Z believing the ground to be firm, treads on it, falls in and is killed. A has committed the offence of culpable homicide.

(ii) A knows Z to be behind a bush. B does not know that A, intending to cause, or knowing it to be likely to cause Z's death, induces B to fire and kill Z. Here B may be guilty of no offence; but A has committed the offence of culpable homicide.

It is important to note that a person who causes bodily injury to another who is labouring under a disorder, disease or bodily infirmity, and thereby accelerates the death of that other, shall be deemed to have caused his death. Also, where death is caused by bodily injury, the person who causes such bodily injury shall be deemed to have caused the death, although by resorting to proper remedies and skilful treatment the death might have been prevented. But causing of the death of a child in the mother's womb is not culpable homicide, it is miscarriage instead. For culpable homicide, any part of that child must have been brought forth, though the child may not have breathed or been completely born.

Culpable Homicide may or may not amount to murder. Culpable Homicide is murder in following cases -

(i) If the act by which the death is caused is done with the intention of causing death, or

(ii) If it is done with the intention of causing such bodily injury as the offender knows to be likely to cause the death of the person to whom the harm is caused, or

(iii) If it is done with the intention of causing bodily injury to any person and the bodily injury intended to be inflicted is sufficient in the ordinary course of nature to cause death, or

(iv) If the person committing the act knows that it is so imminently dangerous that it must, in all probability, cause death, or such bodily injury as is likely to cause death, and commits such act without any excuse for incurring the risk of causing death or such injury as aforesaid.

Thus, Murder is the most heinous of the culpable homicide. And every murder is culpable homicide, but every culpable homicide is not murder. Only when the intention of causing the bodily injury is coupled with the knowledge of the likelihood of such injury causing the death or its sufficiency in ordinary course of nature to cause death, is sufficient for a culpable homicide to amount to murder.

Illustration

(i) A shoots Z with the intention of killing him. Z dies in consequence. A commits murder.

(ii) A intentionally gives Z a sword-cut or club-wound sufficient to cause the death of a man in the ordinary course of nature. Z dies in consequence. Here A is guilty of murder, although he may not have intended to cause Z's death.

Culpable Homicide is not murder in following cases -

11.1. Grave and sudden provocation

Culpable homicide is not murder if the offender, whilst deprived of the power of self-control by grave and sudden provocation, causes the death of the person who gave the provocation or causes the death of any other person by mistake or accident.

Illustrations

(i) A, under the influence of passion excited by a provocation given by Z, intentionally kills Y, Z's child. This is murder, inasmuch as the provocation was not given by the child, and the death of the child was not caused by accident or misfortune in doing an act caused by the provocation.

(ii) Y gives grave and sudden provocation to A. A, on this provocation, fires a pistol at Y, neither intending nor knowing himself to be likely to kill Z, who is near him, but out of sight. A kills Z. Here A has not committed murder, but merely culpable homicide.

11.2. Private defence

Culpable homicide is not murder if the offender in the exercise in good faith of the right of private defence of person or property, exceeds the power given to him by law and causes the death of the person against whom he is exercising such right of defence without premeditation, and without any intention of doing more harm than is necessary for the purpose of such defence.

11.3. Acts of public servants

Culpable homicide is not murder if the offender, being a public servant or aiding a public servant acting for the advancement of public justice, exceeds the powers given to him by law, and causes death by doing an act which he, in good faith, believes to be lawful and necessary for the due discharge of his duty as such public servant and without ill-will towards the person whose death is caused.

11.4. Sudden fight

Culpable homicide is not murder if it is committed without premeditation in a sudden fight in the heat of passion upon a sudden quarrel and without the offender's having taken undue advantage or acted in a cruel or unusual manner.

11.5. Consent

Culpable homicide is not murder when the person whose death is caused, being above the age of eighteen years, suffers death or takes the risk of death with his own consent.

Illustration

(i) A, by instigation, voluntarily causes Z, a person under eighteen years of age to commit suicide. Here, on account of Z's youth, he was incapable of giving consent to his own death; A has therefore abetted murder.

11.6. Transfer of Malice

Take an example, A aims and fires his gun at B. But B moves and evades the bullet. The bullet, instead hits and kills C. Here, though A did not intend to kill C, he is liable for C's murder.

This is called Principal of Transfer of Malice. It states that if a person, by doing anything which he intends or knows to be likely to cause death, commits culpable homicide by causing the death of any person, whose death he neither intends nor knows himself to be likely to cause, the culpable homicide committed by the offender is of the description of which it would have been if he had caused the death of the person whose death he intended or knew himself to he likely to cause.

12. DEATH BY NEGLIGENCE

Law states that whoever causes the death of any person by doing any rash or negligent act not amounting to culpable homicide shall be punished.

The provisions of this section applies when following conditions are fulfiled -

(a) Death of a human being;

(b) The accused caused the death;

(c) The death was caused by the doing of a rash and negligent act, though it did not amount to culpable homicide.

The provision applies to cases where neither there is intention to cause death, nor knowledge that death is likely. Yet, there is some form of mens rea. That is, the person has either acted in rash or negligent manner. If an act is intended to hurt and injure a specific person or object, the perpetrator of the act must be imputed with an intentional act done and cannot amount to a 'rash' and 'negligent' act. Rash means to act hastily as opposed to deliberate act. Negligence, on the other hand, means breach of duty to care that the circumstances call for. Here, the prescribed standard of rashness or negligence is that it must be Gross.

Indian Supreme Court has observed that the concept of negligence differs in civil and criminal law. What may be negligence in civil law may not necessarily be negligence in criminal law. For negligence to amount to an offence, the element of mens rea must be shown to exist and for an act to amount to criminal negligence, the degree of negligence should be much higher, that is, gross or of a very high degree. Negligence that is neither gross nor of a higher degree may provide a ground for action in civil law but cannot form the basis for prosecution.

In cases of Medical Negligence, to prosecute a medical professional under criminal law, it must be shown that the accused did something or failed to do something which in the given facts and circumstances no medical professional in his ordinary senses and prudence would have done or failed to do. And the injury sustained was most likely imminent.

13. DOWRY DEATH

Owing to the peculiar social fabric of the nation, Dowry Death is an India specific offence. Law provides that where the death of a woman is caused by any burns or bodily injury or occurs otherwise than under normal circumstances within seven years of her marriage and it is shown that soon before her death she was subjected to cruelty or harassment by her husband or any relative of her husband for, or in connection with, any demand for dowry, such death shall be called "dowry death", and such husband or relative shall be deemed to have caused her death.

Thus, essential ingredients of the offence of dowry death are -

(a) Death of a woman is caused by any burns or bodily injury or occurs otherwise than under normal circumstances,

(b) Death within seven years of her marriage,

(c) She was subjected to cruelty or harassment by her husband or any relative of her husband,

(d) She was so subjected soon before her death,

(e) Such cruelty or harassment is in connection with any demand for dowry.

14. HURT AND GRIEVOUS HURT

Hurt means causing Bodily pain, Disease or Infirmity to any person.

Grievous hurt means Hurt of any of the following kind -

(a) Emasculation;

(b) Permanent privation of the sight of either eye;

(c) Permanent privation of the hearing of either ear;

(d) Privation of any member or joint;

(e) Destruction or permanent impairing of the powers of any member or joint;

(f) Permanent dis-figuration of the head or face;

(g) Fracture or dislocation of a bone or tooth; or

(h) Any hurt which endangers life or which causes the sufferer to be during the space of twenty days in severe bodily pain, or unable to follow his ordinary pursuits.

Hurt and grievous hurt are punishable if caused voluntarily. Voluntarily means Intentional or with knowledge of likely consequence. But it is not necessary that the hurt be caused in the intended manner alone.

Illustration

(i) A, intending of knowing himself to be likely permanently to disfigure Z's face, gives Z a blow which does not permanently disfigure Z's face, but which causes Z to suffer severe bodily pain for the space of twenty days. A has voluntarily caused grievous hurt.

15. WRONGFUL RESTRAINT AND WRONGFUL CONFINEMENT

Wrongful restraint means voluntarily obstructing any person so as to prevent him from proceeding in any direction in which he has a right to proceed.

Illustration

(i) A obstructs a path along which Z has a right to pass. Z is thereby prevented from passing. A wrongfully restrains Z.

Wrongful confinement means wrongfully restraining any person in such a manner as to prevent him from proceedings beyond certain circumscribing limits.

Illustrations

(i) A causes Z to go within a walled space, and locks Z in Z is thus prevented from proceeding in any direction beyond the circumscribing line of wall. A wrongfully confines Z.

(ii) A places men with firearms at the outlets of a building, and tells Z that they will fire at Z if Z attempts leave the building. A wrongfully confines Z.

Thus, restraint is in respect of a particular direction, while confinement is within certain boundaries or in respect of all directions.

16. CRIMINAL FORCE AND ASSAULT

Before we understand criminal force and assault, we need to understand Force. In physics, Force means a push or a pull. Legally, too, force has similar connotation. A person is said to use force to another if he causes -

(a) motion, change of motion, or cessation of motion to that other, or

(b) to any substance such motion, or change of motion, or cessation of motion as brings that substance into contact with

(i) any part of that other's body, or

(ii) anything which that other is wearing or carrying, or

(iii) anything so situated that such contact affects that other's sense of feeling.

Provided that he does so by -

(a) his own bodily power,

(b) disposing any substance in such a manner that the motion or change or cessation of motion takes place without any further act on his part, or on the part of any other person,

(c) inducing any animal to move, to change its motion, or to cease to move.

16.1. Criminal Force

Criminal force means intentionally using force to any person, without that person's consent, in order to the committing of any offence, or intending by the use of such force to cause, or knowing it to be likely that by the use of such force he will cause injury, fear or annoyance to the person to whom the force is used, is said to use criminal force to that other.

Essentials of Criminal Force

(i) Use of Force,

(ii) Intentionally,

(iii) Without consent,

(iv) In order to commit any offence, or

(v) Intention to cause or knowledge that it is likely to cause -

(a) injury,

(b) fear or

(c) annoyance to the person to whom the force is used.

Illustrations

(i) Z is sitting in a moored boat on a river. A unfastens the moorings, and thus intentionally causes the boat to drift down the stream. Here A intentionally causes motion to Z, and he does this by disposing substances in such a manner that the motion is produced without any other action on any person's part. A has therefore intentionally used force to Z.

(ii) Z is riding in a chariot. A lashes Z's horses, and thereby causes them to quicken their pace. Here A has caused change of motion to Z by inducing the animals to change their motion. A has therefore used force to Z.

(iii) Z is bathing. A pours boiling water into the bath. Here A intentionally by his own bodily power causes such motion in the boiling water as brings that water into contact with Z, or with other water so situated that such contact must affect Z's sense of feeling; A has therefore intentionally used force to Z.

If, in any of the above examples, the force is used without consent, and in order to the committing of any offence, or intending or knowing it to be likely that this use of force will cause injury, fear or annoyance, the force used is criminal force.

(iv) Z is riding in a palanquin. A, intending to rob Z, seizes the pole and stops the palanquin. Here A has caused cessation of motion to Z, and he has done this by his own bodily power. A has therefore used force to Z; and as A has acted thus intentionally, without Z's consent, in order to the commission of an offence. A has used criminal force to Z.

(v) A throws a stone, intending or knowing it to be likely that the stone will be thus brought into contact with Z, or with Z's clothes, or with something carried by Z, or that it will strike water and dash up the water against Z's clothes or something carried by Z. Here, if the throwing of the stone produce the effect of causing any substance to come into contact with Z, or Z's clothes, A has used force to Z, and if he did so without Z's consent, intending thereby to injure, frighten or annoy Z, he has used criminal force to Z.

(vi) A incites a dog to spring upon Z, without Z's consent. Here, if A intends to cause injury, fear or annoyance to Z, he uses criminal force to Z.

16.2. Assault

Assault is means show of criminal force rather than actual use of it. Assault is defined as making any gesture, or any preparation with intention or knowledge that it is likely that such gesture or preparation will cause any person present to apprehend that he who makes that gesture or preparation is about to use criminal force to that person.

Essentials of Assault

(i) Gesture or Preparation

(ii) Intentional or with knowledge that it is likely

(iii) To raise apprehension of

(iv) Use of Criminal Forced

(v) Mere words do not amount to an assault. But words accompanied with gestures or preparation may amount to an assault.

Illustrations

(i) A shakes his fist at Z, intending or knowing it to be likely that he may thereby cause Z to believe that A is about to strike Z. A has committed an assault.

(ii) A begins to unloose the muzzle of a ferocious dog, intending or knowing it to be likely that he may thereby cause Z to believe that he is about to cause the dog to attack Z. A has committed an assault upon Z.

(iii) A takes up a stick, saying to Z, "I will give you a beating". Here, though the words used by A could in no case amount to an assault, and though the mere gesture, unaccompanied by any other circumstances, might not amount to an assault. The gesture explained by the words may amount to an assault.

17. KIDNAPPING AND ABDUCTION

17.1. Kidnapping

Kidnapping is of two kinds -

(a) Kidnapping from India,

(b) Kidnapping from lawful guardianship.

Kidnapping from India means -

(a) Conveying any person,

(b) Beyond the limits of India,

(c) Without the consent of that person or a person legally authorised to consent on his behalf.

Kidnapping from lawful guardianship means -

(a) Taking or enticing,

(b) Any minor - Male under 16 years or Female under 18 years, or

(c) Any person of unsound mind,

(d) Out of the keeping of Lawful guardian,

(e) Without the consent of a lawful guardian.

Illustration

(i) A (unrelated to G) offers G (a minor) a chocolate to enter her car. G enters her car. A has kidnapped G.

The offence of kidnapping is one against guardianship and is committed as soon as the minor is taken out of lawful guardianship. Further, it is no defence that the accused did not know the victim to be minor or that he honestly believed the victim to be major. This is because the offence of kidnapping is a strict liability offence and is punishable sans mens rea.

17.2. Abduction

A person is said to abduct another if he by -

(a) Force compels, or

(b) Any deceitful means induces,

(c) Any person to go from any place

Abduction is thus fraudulent or forceful removal from a place. And, the offence may be committed against person of any age. Abduction, in its nature, is a continuing offence.

18. SEXUAL OFFENCE

18.1. Rape

A man is said to commit Rape if he -

(a) penetrates his penis, to any extent, into the vagina, mouth, urethra or anus of a woman or makes her to do so with him or any other person; or

(b) inserts, to any extent, any object or a part of the body, not being the penis, into the vagina, the urethra or anus of a woman or makes her to do so with him or any other person; or

(c) manipulates any part of the body of a woman so as to cause penetration into the vagina, urethra, anus or any part of body of such woman or makes her to do so with him or any other person; or

(d) applies his mouth to the vagina, anus, urethra of a woman or makes her to do so with him or any other person,

under any of the following circumstances -

(i) Against her will.

(ii) Without her consent.

(iii) With her consent, when her consent has been obtained by putting her or any person in whom she is interested, in fear of death or of hurt.

(iv) With her consent, when the man knows that he is not her husband and that her consent is given because she believes that he is another man to whom she is or believes herself to be lawfully married.

(v) With her consent when, at the time of giving such consent, by reason of unsoundness of mind or intoxication or the administration by him personally or through another of any stupefying or unwholesome substance, she is unable to understand the nature and consequences of that to which she gives consent.

(vi) With or without her consent, when she is under eighteen years of age.

(vii) When she is unable to communicate consent.

A medical procedure or intervention shall not constitute rape. Also, sexual intercourse by a man with his wife, the wife not being under fifteen years of age, is not rape. Consent of a girl below the age of eighteen is immaterial. A conviction on a charge of rape on the uncorroborated testimony of the victim / prosecutrix is legal. And the mere fact that a victim / prosecutrix was of loose moral character and was used to sexual intercourse, cannot be used to disbelieve her statement.

19. UNNATURAL OFFENCE

Unnatural Offence means voluntarily having carnal intercourse against the order of nature with any man, woman or animal.

20. THEFT

Whoever, intending to take dishonestly any movable property out of the possession of any person without that person's consent, moves that property in order to such taking, is said to commit theft.

Thus, essential ingredients of theft are -

(a) Take,

(b) Dishonestly,

(c) Any movable property,

(d) Out of possession of any person,

(e) Without his consent,

(f) Moves that property.

Illustration

(i) A cuts down a tree on Z's ground, with the intention of dishonestly taking the tree out of Z's possession without Z's consent. Here, as soon as A has severed the tree in order to such taking, he has committed theft.

(ii) A puts a bait for dogs in his pocket, and thus induces Z's dog to follow it. Here, if A's intention be dishonestly to take the dog out of Z's possession without Z's consent, A has committed theft as soon as Z's dog has begun to follow A.

(iii) A meets a bullock carrying a box of treasure. He drives the bullock in a certain direction, in order that he may dishonestly take the treasure. As soon as the bullock begins to move, A has committed theft of the treasure.

(iv) Z, going on a journey, entrusts his plate to A, the keeper of a warehouse, till Z shall return. A carries the plate to a goldsmith and sells it. Here the plate was not in Z's possession. It could not therefore be taken out of Z's possession, and A has not committed theft, though he may have committed criminal breach of trust.

(v) A finds a ring belonging to Z on a table in the house which Z occupies. Here the ring is in Z's possession, and if A dishonestly removes it, A commits theft.

(vi) A finds a ring lying on the highroad, not in the possession of any person. A, by taking it, commits no theft, though he may later commit criminal misappropriation of property.

(vii) A sees a ring belonging to Z lying on a table in Z's house. Not venturing to misappropriate the ring immediately for fear of search and detection, A hides the ring in a place where it is highly improbable that it will ever be found by Z, with the intention of taking the ring from the hiding place and selling it when the loss is forgotten. Here A, at the time of first moving the ring, commits theft.

(viii) A delivers his watch to Z, a jeweller, to be regulated. Z carries it to his shop. A, not owing to the jeweller any debt for which the jeweller might lawfully detain the watch as a security, enters the shop openly, takes his watch by force out of Z's hand, and carries it away. Here A, though he may have committed criminal trespass and assault, has not committed theft, inasmuch as what he did was not done dishonestly.

(ix) If A owes money to Z for repairing the watch, and if Z retains the watch lawfully as a security for the debt, and A takes the watch out of Z's possession, with the intention of depriving Z of the property as a security for his debt, he commits theft, inasmuch as he takes it dishonestly.

(x) Again, if A, having pawned his watch to Z, takes it out of Z's possession without Z's consent, not having paid what he borrowed on the watch, he commits theft, though the watch is his own property inasmuch as he takes it dishonestly.

(xi) A takes an article belonging to Z out of Z's possession without Z's consent, with the intention of keeping it until he obtains money from Z as a reward for its restoration. Here A takes dishonestly; A has therefor committed theft.

(xii) A, being on friendly terms with Z, goes into Z's library in Z's absence, and takes away a book without Z's express consent for the purpose merely of reading it, and with the intention of returning it. Here, it is probable that A may have conceived that he had Z's implied consent to use Z's book. If this was A's impression, A has not committed theft.

(xiii) A asks charity from Z's wife. She gives A money, food and clothes, which A knows to belong to Z her husband. Here it is probable that A may conceive that Z's wife is authorised to give away alms. If this was A's impression, A has not committed theft.

(xiv) A is the paramour of Z's wife. She gives a valuable property, which A knows to belong to her husband Z, and to be such property as she has not authority from Z to give. If A takes the property dishonestly, he commits theft.

(xv) A, in good faith, believing property belonging to Z to be A's own property, takes that property out of B's possession. Here, as A does not take dishonestly, he does not commit theft.

21. EXTORTION

Whoever intentionally puts any person in fear of any injury to that person, or to any other, and thereby dishonestly induces the person so put in fear to deliver any property or valuable security, or anything signed or sealed which may be converted into a valuable security, commits "extortion".

Thus, essential ingredients of Extortion are -

(a) Dishonest Intention,

(b) Put any person in fear of any injury,

(c) Induce him,

(d) Deliver any property or valuable security or anything signed or sealed which may be converted into a valuable security.

Offences such as Blackmail and demand of protection money are offences included in extortion. It is important to note that subject matter of theft is movable property only, but subject matter of extortion may also be an immovable property.

Illustration

(i) A threatens to publish a defamatory libel concerning Z unless Z gives him money. He thus induces Z to give him money. A has committed extortion.

(ii) A threatens Z that he will keep Z's child in wrongful confinement, unless Z will sign and deliver to A a promissory note binding Z to pay certain monies to A. Z signs and delivers the note. A has committed extortion.

(iii) A, by putting Z in fear of grievous hurt, dishonestly induces Z to sign or affix his seal to a blank paper and deliver it to A. Z signs and delivers the paper to A. Here, as the paper so signed may be converted into a valuable security, A has committed extortion.

22. ROBBERY

Robbery is aggravated form of theft or extortion. Each robbery must be either a theft or an extortion.

Theft is "Robbery" if, in order to the committing of the theft, or in committing the theft, or in carrying away or attempting to carry away property obtained by the theft, the offender, for that end voluntarily causes or attempts to cause to any person death or hurt or wrongful restraint, or fear of instant death or of instant hurt, or of instant wrongful restraint.

Extortion is "Robbery" if the offender, at the time of committing the extortion, is in the presence of the person put in fear, and commits the extortion by putting that person in fear of instant death, of instant hurt, or of instant wrongful restraint to that person or to some other person, and, by so putting in fear, induces the person so put in fear then and there to deliver up the thing extorted.

Thus, Robbery is,

Theft + Cause or Attempt + Death or Hurt or Wrongful Restraint or Instant Fear of any of them

or

Extortion + Fear of Instant Death or Instant Hurt or Instant Wrongful Restraint

Illustration

(i) A holds Z down, and fraudulently takes Z's money and jewels from Z's clothes, without Z's consent. Here A has committed theft, and, in order to the committing of that theft, has voluntarily caused wrongful restraint to Z. A has therefore committed robbery.

(ii) A meets Z on the high road, shows a pistol, and demands Z's purse. Z, in consequence, surrenders his purse. Here A has extorted the purse from Z by putting him in fear of instant hurt, and being at the time of committing the extortion in his presence. A has therefore committed robbery.

(iii) A obtains property from Z by saying, "Your child is in the hands of my gang, and will be put to death unless you send us ten thousand rupees". This is extortion, and punishable as such. It is not robbery, unless Z is put in fear of the instant death of his child.

23. DISHONEST MISAPPROPRIATION OF PROPERTY

IPC does not define misappropriation, but it can be understood in common parlance as an unlawful appropriation of funds or thing or conversion to one's own use any movable property.

Illustrations

(i) A takes property belonging to Z out of Z's possession, in good faith believing at the time when he takes it, that the property belongs to himself. A is not guilty of theft; but if A, after discovering his mistake, dishonestly appropriates the property to his own use, he is guilty of dishonest misappropriation of property.

(ii) A, being on friendly terms with Z, goes into Z's library in Z's absence, and takes away a book without Z's express consent. Here, if A was under the impression that he had Z's implied consent to take the book for the purpose of reading it, A has not committed theft. But, if A afterwards sells the book for his own benefit, he is guilty of dishonest misappropriation of property.

(iii) A and B, being, joint owners of a horse, A takes the horse out of B's possession, intending to use it. Here, as A has a right to use the horse, he does not dishonestly misappropriate it. But, if A sells the horse and appropriates the whole proceeds to his own use, he is guilty of dishonest misappropriation of property.

A dishonest misappropriation for a time only is a misappropriation within the meaning of this section. Also, a person who finds property not in the possession of any other person, and takes such property for the purpose of protecting if for, or of restoring it to, the owner does not take or misappropriate it dishonestly, and is not guilty of an offence. However, he is guilty of the offence above defined, if he appropriates it to his own use, when he knows or has the means of discovering the owner, or before he has used reasonable means to discover and give notice to the owner and has kept the property a reasonable time to enable the owner to claim it.

Illustration

(i) A finds a government promissory note belonging to Z, bearing a blank endorsement. A knowing that the note belongs to Z, pledges it with a banker as a security for a loan, intending at a future time to restore it to Z. A is guilty of dishonest misappropriation of property.

(ii) A finds a rupee on the road, not knowing to whom the rupee belongs. A picks up the rupee. Here, A has not committed the above offence.

(iii) A finds a letter on the road, containing a bank note. From the address and contents of the letter, he learns to whom the note belongs. He appropriates the note. He is guilty of dishonest misappropriation of property.

(iv) A sees Z drop his purse with money in it. A picks up the purse with the intention of restoring it to Z, but afterwards appropriates it to his own use. A is guilty of dishonest misappropriation of property.

24. CRIMINAL BREACH OF TRUST

Whoever, being in any manner entrusted with property, or with any dominion over property, dishonestly misappropriates or converts to his own use that property, or dishonestly uses or disposes of that property in violation of any direction of law prescribing the mode in which such trust is to be discharged, or of any legal contract, express or implied, which he has made touching the discharge of such trust, or wilfully suffers any other person so to do, commits "criminal breach of trust".

From the definition, the ingredients of the offence are -

(i) Person is entrusted with property,

(ii) He does any of the following acts with the said property,

(a) Dishonestly misappropriates, or

(b) Converts to his own use, or

(c) Dishonestly uses or disposes of that property in violation of any direction of law or legal contract, or

(d) Wilfully suffers any other person so to do

In simple words, where any sum of money is said to have been embezzled and it is proved that he had received the sum but he fails to account for the same, the offence of criminal breach of trust is established. That is, once the entrustment is proved, it is for the accused to prove how the property entrusted was dealt with.

25. RECEIVING STOLEN PROPERTY

Property, the possession whereof has been transferred by theft, or by extortion, or by robbery, and property which has been criminally misappropriated or in respect of which criminal breach of trust has been committed, is designated as "stolen property", whether the transfer has been made, or the misappropriation or breach of trust has been committed, within or without India. But, if such property subsequently comes into the possession of a person legally entitled to the possession thereof, it then ceases to be stolen property.

Thus, stolen property means any property that has been subject of -

(a) Theft,

(b) Extortion,

(c) Robbery,

(d) Criminal Misappropriation,

(e) Criminal Breach of Trust,

anywhere in the world.

Such property ceases to be stolen property, if it comes into possession of rightful person. Note that rightful person is not necessarily the owner, but the person entitled to possession, as we have already seen that an owner may himself commit theft also.

Law prohibits offences like dishonestly receiving stolen property, habitually dealing in them or voluntarily assisting in concealment of a stolen property.

26. CHEATING

Whoever, by deceiving any person, fraudulently or dishonestly induces the person so deceived to deliver any property to any person, or to consent that any person shall retain any property, or intentionally induces the person so deceived to do or omit to do anything which he would not do or omit if he were not so deceived, and which act or omission causes or is likely to cause damage or harm to that person in body, mind, reputation or property, is said to "cheat".

Thus, ingredients of Cheating are -

(a) Inducement,

(b) Dishonest or Fraudulent,

(c) Inducing that person to -

(i) Deliver any property to any person; or

(ii) Consent that any person shall retain any property, or

(iii) to do or omit to do anything which he would not do or omit if he were not so deceived,

(iv) Act or omission causes or is likely to cause damage or harm to that person in body, mind, reputation, or property.

Illustrations

(i) A, by putting a counterfeit mark on an article, intentionally deceives Z into a belief that this article was made by a certain celebrated manufacturer, and thus dishonestly induces Z to buy and pay for the article. A cheats.

(ii) A, by exhibiting to Z a false sample of an article intentionally deceives Z into believing that the article corresponds with the sample, and thereby dishonestly induces Z to buy and pay for the article. A cheats.

(iii) A, by pledging as diamond articles which he knows are not diamonds, intentionally deceives Z, and thereby dishonestly induces Z to lend money. A cheats.

(iv) A Intentionally deceives Z into a belief that A means to repay any money that Z may lend to him and thereby dishonestly induces Z to lend him money, A not intending to repay it. A cheats.

(v) A intentionally deceives Z into a belief that A means to deliver to Z a certain quantity of indigo plant which he does not intend to deliver, and thereby dishonestly induces Z to advance money upon the faith of such delivery. A cheats; but if A, at the time of obtaining the money, intends to deliver the indigo plant, and afterwards breaks his contract and does not deliver it, he does not cheat, but is liable only to a civil action for breach of contract.

(vi) A sells and conveys an estate to B. A, knowing that in consequence of such sale he has no right to the property, sells or mortgages the same to Z, without disclosing the fact of the previous sale and conveyance to B, and receives the purchase or mortgage money from Z. A cheats.

(vii) A cheats by pretending to be a certain rich banker of the same name. A cheats by personation.

(viii) A cheats by pretending to be B, a person who is deceased. A cheats by personation.

27. MISCHIEF

Whoever with intent to cause, or knowing that he is likely to cause, wrongful loss or damage to the public or to any person, causes the destruction of any property, or any such change in any property or in the situation thereof as destroys or diminishes its value or utility, or affects it injuriously, commits "mischief".

The ingredients of the offence of Mischief are -

(a) Intention or Knowledge of likelihood,

(b) Wrongful loss or damage to Public or Person,

(c) Cause

    (i) Destruction of any Property, or

    (ii) Diminish its value or utility, or

    (iii) Affect it injuriously.

It is not essential to the offence of mischief that the offender should intend to cause loss or damage to the owner of the property injured or destroyed. It is sufficient if he intends to cause, or knows that he is likely to cause, wrongful loss or damage to any person by injuring any property, whether it belongs to that person or not. Also, Mischief may be committed by an act affecting property belonging to the person himself, wholly or partly.

Illustrations

(i) A voluntarily burns a valuable security belonging to Z intending to cause wrongful loss to Z. A has committed mischief.

(ii) A voluntarily throws into a river a ring belonging to Z, with the intention of thereby causing wrongful loss to Z. A has committed mischief.

(iii) A, knowing that his effects are about to be taken in execution in order to satisfy a debt due from him to Z, destroys those effects, with the intention of thereby preventing Z from obtaining satisfaction of the debt, and of thus causing damage to Z. A has committed mischief.

(iv) A having insured a ship, voluntarily causes the same to be cast away, with the intention of causing damage to the underwriters. A has committed mischief.

(v) A, having joint property with Z in a horse, shoots the horse, intending thereby to cause wrongful loss to Z. A has committed mischief.

(vi) A causes cattle to enter upon a field belonging to Z, intending to cause and knowing that he is likely to cause damage to Z's crop. A has committed mischief.

28. CRIMINAL TRESPASS

Whoever enters into or upon property in the possession of another with intent to commit an offence or to intimidate, insult or annoy any person in possession of such property, or having lawfully entered into or upon such property, unlawfully remains there with intent thereby to intimidate, insult or annoy any such person, or with intent to commit an offence, is said to commit "criminal trespass".

Thus, Criminal Trespass consists in -

(a) Unlawful Entry, or

(b) Having lawfully entered, remaining unlawfully there,

(c) Intent to intimidate, insult or annoy any person, or commit an offence.

Criminal Trespass may be of varying degrees, some of which are -

(i) House Trespass.

(ii) Lurking House Trespass.

(iii) Lurking House Trespass by Night.

(iv) House Breaking.

(v) House Breaking by Night.

29. OFFENCES RELATING TO DOCUMENTS

29.1. Forgery

Whoever makes any false document or false electronic record or part of a document or electronic record, with intent to cause damage or injury, to the public or to any person, or to support any claim or title, or to cause any person to part with property, or to enter into any express or implied contract, or with intent to commit fraud or that fraud may be committed, commits forgery.

Thus, forgery consists in -

(a) Makes any false document, electronic record or its part with intent to -

(i) Cause damage or injury to the public or to any person, or

(ii) Support any claim or title, or

(iii) Cause any person to part with property, or

(iv) Enter into any express or implied contract, or

(v) Commit fraud

As far as Making False Documents is concerned, it is any of the following acts -

(a) Dishonestly or fraudulently makes or executes a document with the intention of causing it to be believed that such document was made or executed by some other person, or by the authority of some other person,

(b) Dishonestly or fraudulently, alters or cancels a document in any material part, without lawful authority, after it has been made or executed by either himself or any other person;

(c) Dishonestly or fraudulently causes any person to sign, execute or alter a document knowing that such person could not by reason of Unsoundness of mind, Intoxication, or Deception practised upon him, know the contents of the document or the nature of the alteration.

A man's signature of his own name may, under certain circumstances, amount to forgery. Also, the making of a false document in the name of a fictitious person, intending it to be believed that the document was made by a real person, or in the name of a deceased person, intending it to be believed that the document was made by the person in his lifetime, may amount to forgery.

Illustrations

(i) A has a letter of credit upon B for rupees 10,000, written by Z. A, in order to defraud B, adds cipher to the 10,000, and makes the sum 1,00,000 intending that it may be believed by B that Z so wrote the letter. A has committed forgery.

(ii) A, without Z's authority, affixes Z's seal to a document purporting to be a conveyance of an estate from Z to A, with the intention of selling the estate to B and thereby of obtaining from B the purchase-money. A has committed forgery.

(iii) A picks up a cheque on a banker signed by B, payable to bearer, but without any sum having been inserted in the cheque. A fraudulently fills up the cheque by inserting the sum of ten thousand rupees. A commits forgery.

(iv) A leaves with B, his agent, a cheque on a banker, signed by A, without inserting the sum payable and authorizes B to fill up the cheque by inserting a sum not exceeding ten thousand rupees for the purpose of making certain payments. B fraudulently fills up the cheque by inserting the sum of twenty thousand rupees. B commits forgery.

(v) A draws a bill of exchange on himself in the name of B without B's authority, intending to discount it as a genuine bill with a banker and intending to take up the bill on its maturity. Here, as A draws the bill with intent to deceive the banker by leading him to suppose that he had the security of B, and thereby to discount the bill, A is guilty of forgery.

(vi) Z's will contains these words — "I direct that all my remaining property be equally divided between A, B and C." A dishonestly scratches out B's name, intending that it may be believed that the whole was left to himself and C. A has committed forgery.

(vii) A endorses a Government promissory note and makes it payable to Z or his order by writing on the bill the words "Pay to Z or his order" and signing the endorsement. B dishonestly erases the words "Pay to Z or his order", and thereby converts the special endorsement into a blank endorsement. B commits forgery.

(viii) A sells and conveys an estate to Z. A afterwards, in order to defraud Z of his estate, executes a conveyance of the same estate to B, dated six months earlier than the date of the conveyance to Z, intending it to be believed that he had conveyed the estate to B before he conveyed it to Z. A has committed forgery.

(ix) Z dictates his will to A. A intentionally writes down a different legatee named by Z, and by representing to Z that he has prepared the will according to his instructions, induces Z to sign the will. A has committed forgery.

(x) A signs his own name to a bill of exchange, intending that it may be believed that the bill was drawn by another person of the same name. A has committed forgery.

(xi) A writes the word "accepted" on a piece of paper and signs it with Z's name, in order that B may afterwards write on the paper a bill of exchange drawn by B upon Z, and negotiate the bill as though it had been accepted by Z. A is guilty of forgery; and if B, knowing the fact, draws the bill upon the paper pursuant to A's intention, B is also guilty of forgery.

(xii) A, a trader, in anticipation of insolvency, lodges effects with B for A's benefit, and with intent to defraud his creditors; and in order to give a colour to the transaction, writes a promissory note binding himself to pay to B a sum for value received, and antedates the note, intending that it may be believed to have been made before A was on the point of insolvency. A has committed forgery.

(xiii) A draws a bill of exchange upon a fictitious person, and fraudulently accepts the bill in the name of such fictitious person with intent to negotiate it. A commits forgery.

30. DEFAMATION

Defamation, whether slander or libel, is both a tort and a crime under the Indian Law.

Whoever by words either spoken or intended to be read, or by signs or by visible representations, makes or publishes any imputation concerning any person intending to harm, or knowing or having reason to believe that such imputation will harm, the reputation of such person is said to defame that person. Even an imputation expressed ironically may amount to defamation. Such imputations are called innuendo.

For an imputation to be defamatory, it should lower the moral or intellectual character of a person in the estimation of others, or lower his character in respect of his caste or calling, or lower his credit, or cause it to be believed that his body is in a loathsome state, or in a state generally considered as disgraceful.

Illustrations

(a) A says - "Z is an honest man; he never stole B's watch", intending to cause it to be believed that Z did steal B's watch. This is defamation, unless it fall within one of the exceptions.

(b) A draws a picture of Z running away with B's watch, intending it to be believed that Z stole B's watch. This is defamation, unless it fall within one of the exceptions.

30.1. Exceptions to Defamation

Based on the larger public good, the following acts are exceptions specially carved out of defamation -

(a) Imputation of truth which public good requires to be made or published.

(b) Public conduct of public servants.

(c) Conduct of any person touching any public question.

(d) Publication of reports of proceedings of courts.

(e) Merits of case decided in Court or conduct of witnesses and others concerned.

(f) Merits of public performance.

(g) Censure passed in good faith by person having lawful authority over another.

(h) Accusation preferred in good faith to authorised person.

(i) Imputation made in good faith by person for protection of his or other's interests.

(j) Caution intended for good of person to whom conveyed or for public good.

Illustrations

(a) A writer who publishes a book, or an actor or singer who appears on a public stage, submits that book, acting or singing to the judgment of the public.

(b) A says of a book published by Z - "Z's book is indecent; Z must be a man of impure mind." A is within the exception.

(c) But if A says - "I am not surprised that Z's book is foolish and indecent, for he is a weak man and a libertine." A is not within this exception, inasmuch as the opinion which he expresses of Z's character is an opinion not founded on Z's book.

(d) A, a shopkeeper, says to his manager B – "Don't sell anything to Z unless he pays you ready money, for I have no opinion of his honesty." A is within the exception, if he has made this imputation on Z in good faith for the protection of his own interests.

31. ATTEMPT OF OFFENCE

Law does not define attempt, but it can be understood as an act of trying. A person is said to commit attempt of an offence when he, with the intention or knowledge requisite for committing it, does any act towards its commission. That act so done is closely connected with, and proximate to the commission of the offence, and the act fails in its object because of facts not known to him or because of circumstances beyond his control.

In simple terms, an attempt of offence is one which would be ordinarily successful but fails otherwise than due to the effort of the perpetrator.

31.1. Stages of Crime

A Crime, in its commission, under goes various stages, which are as follows -

(i) **Motive:** Motive is the driving force behind the crime. It is the reason for or ends with which the crime is committed. Motiveless crime is a rarity.

(ii) **Intention**: Intention refers to the psychology of the criminal committing the offence. It is the mental element in the crime.

(iii) **Preparation**: Preparation means devising a plan or arranging any necessary means for successful commission of offence. Ordinarily, preparation of an offence is not punishable, because of lack of element of injury. And difficulty of proof. However, notable exceptions - Preparation to wage war against Government of India and Preparation to commit dacoity are punishable offences.

(iv) **Attempt**: Attempt means an accurate move towards committing the envisioned crime after having made the arrangements. Once an attempt is executed, the perpetrator cannot alter its discourse or retort to its initial status.

(v) **Actual Commission of crime:** The actual commission of the crime leads to Criminal liability. If the perpetrator ensues in his attempt, the offence is committed. If missed, it is regarded as an attempt.

31.2. Theories of Attempt

It is often difficult to spell out exactly as to what is sufficient to amount to an attempt. For this, various theories have been propounded, which as as follows -

(a) The Proximity Rule

The proximity rule is based on the principle that nobody deserves punishment for thought. The Proximity Rule examines as to how close the perpetrator was to commission of the offence and whether the gap (if any) is a deliberate one. Under this rule, the act left to be done is analysed, and the attempt is made once nothing was left to be done by the perpetrator.

(b) Locus Poenitentiae (Doctrine of Repentance)

This theory states that a person cannot be charged for an attempt if he is in position to give up or abandon his plan out of his own accord after the formation of Mens rea.

This doctrine deals with the cases where an individual has made all the preparation to commit the offence but decided against it at the last moment. Thus, it says that a last minute withdrawal before commission is sufficient to avoid criminal liability.

(c) The Equivocality Test

Equivocality means susceptible of double interpretation, or allowing possibility of several meanings.

The Equivocality Test is used to distinguish between the stages of preparation and attempt. This test examines the progress towards the commission and states that the attempt to commit a specific offence is constituted when the accused does an act which is a step towards the commission of that offence and doing of such an act cannot reasonably be regarded as having another purpose than the commission of that specific offence.. Thus, under this theory for an act to be attempt it must be unequivocally criminal.

(d) Substantial Steps Test

This test states that in addition to intent, it must be established that the perpetrator took a substantial step beyond mere preparation to commit the crime. Thus, mere discussion or contemplation of crime is not enough. Rather, the act must be such that it leads the perpetrator toward the successful completion of the offence, even though it is not fully executed.

(e) Attempting an Impossible Act

A person may be guilty of attempt even when the commission is rendered impossible due to factors beyond control of that person. This theory negates a possible defence of the accused but is often criticised for complexity.

For example, it is an attempt if A press trigger of an unloaded gun aiming and intending to kill B, not knowing that the gun is unloaded. But it is not an attempt if A shoots at B's office chair not knowing it to be unoccupied.

31.3. Conclusion

It is not just the act but also the guilt that is punished. Hence, not only a successful but also an unsuccessful attempt to commit a criminal offence is punishable by law. But the act must be sufficient to be regarded as an attempt before criminal liability may be attached to it.

CIVIL PROCEDURE

1. Introduction

The law relating to conduct of civil cases is contained in Code of Civil Procedure, 1908 (or CPC). It is an elaborate and extensive enactment that deals with jurisdiction of Civil Court, Institution and Conduct of Civil Cases, Appeals and Executions of Judgments and Decrees, etc.

Having regard to the length and breath of the statute, only few important aspects of Civil Procedure are discussed herein for the sake of lucidity.

1.1. Stages in Civil Suit

A Civil Suit is instituted by filing of Plaint. Once plaint is registered, the Court issues summons to the defendant, who may then appear and contest the claim by filing his written statement.

The Court, then, examines whether the case is fit for any Alternate Dispute Resolution such as Arbitration, Mediation, Conciliation. If the matter is referred to ADR and is returned unsettled or if the matter is not fit for ADR, the Court proceeds to frame issues in the matter.

Plaintiff Evidence, followed by Defendant Evidence is recorded. After hearing the arguments, the Court proceeds to pronounce its Judgment, based on which a Decree is drawn.

The person in whose favour a decree has been passed is called Decree-Holder. The person against whom a decree has been passed is called Judgment-Debtor.

A Judgment-Debtor has further remedies in form of Review, Revision and Appeal, while Decree-Holder may file for execution, if the obligation under the decree is not voluntarily fulfilled by the judgment-debtor.

2. SUIT OF CIVIL NATURE

A Civil Court has jurisdiction to try all suits of civil nature unless expressly or impliedly barred.

The word 'civil' is not defined by the statute. Its dictionary meaning is pertaining to private rights and remedies of a citizen as distinguished from criminal, political, etc. The word 'nature' means fundamental characteristic. Thus, a civil nature suit is one where the principal question relates to the determination of civil right and its enforcement. Political and religious questions are not covered under this expression.

For example, Suits relating to rights to property, right of worship, right to share in offerings, damages for civil wrongs, specific performance of contracts, damages for breach of contracts, specific relief, restitution of conjugal rights, dissolution of marriages, rent, wrongful dismissal from service and for salaries, etc. are suits of civil nature. While suits involving principally caste questions, purely religious rites or ceremonies, for upholding mere dignity or honor, for recovery of voluntary payments or offerings, against expulsions from caste, are not suits of civil nature.

A suit where the principal question relates to civil nature does not cease to be a suit of a civil nature merely because the adjudication incidentally involves determination as to caste question or to religious rights and ceremonies. It is also immaterial whether any fees is attached to the office or not and whether the office is attached to any religious place or not.

3. BAR OF SUIT

3.1. Res sub-judice

Res sub-judice literally means right under judicial consideration. To avoid multiplicity of proceedings and conflicting judgments in respect of same issue by different courts of concurrent jurisdiction, law provides for the principle of res sub-judice.

It states that two parallel proceedings cannot be carried out simultaneously in respect of same subject matter. No Court shall proceed with the trial of a suit if the matter in issue is also directly and substantially in issue in a previously instituted suit between the same parties. It is the latter of the two suits that is stayed.

For example, Wife A filed a suit for divorce and custody of minor child against husband B. Subsequently, B filed another suit for custody of minor child against B. Second suit is liable to be stayed under section 10 of CPC,1908.

Although, a suit pending in a Foreign Court does not bar institution of suit in India.

3.2. Res Judicata

Res Judicata means 'right decided'. It is important that judicial decision should attain finality. Thus, a matter once adjudicated by competent court should not be open to similar adjudication by same Court or Court of concurrent jurisdiction.

The rule states that no Court shall try any suit or issue in which the matter directly and substantially in issue has been directly and substantially in issue in a former suit between the same parties litigating under the same title, in a court competent to try such subsequent suit or the suit in which such issue has been subsequently raised, and has been heard and finally decided by such Court.

For example, A sues B for breach of contract. The suit is dismissed. A subsequently sues B for damages for breach of contract on the same contract. Second suit is barred by Res Judicata.

But where, A sues B for possession of property alleging that it has come to his share on partition of joint family property. B's contention that the partition has not taken place is upheld by the court and the suit is dismissed. A subsequent suit by A against B for partition of joint family property is not barred.

Essential Conditions for applicability -

(i) The matter directly & substantially in issue in subsequent suit was directly and substantially in issue in the former suit.

(ii) The former suit must have been between the same parties or between their representatives.

(iii) The parties to the suit must have litigated under the same title in the former suit.

(iv) The court which decided the former suit was competent to try the subsequent suit.

(v) The matter was heard and finally decided by the court.

3.3. Constructive res judicata

Constructive res judicata is a species of the genus res judicata. Ordinarily, for application of res judicata, the matter should have been directly and substantially in issue in a former suit.

However, having regard to the dispute, there may be matters which the party might and ought to have raised before the Court as a ground of attack or defence, but they fail to do so. In such cases, it is deemed that such matter was directly and substantially in issue in former suit, and that it was also heard and decided. Thus, it is construed that the suit is barred by res Judicata.

For example, A sues B for possession of property on the basis of ownership. The suit is dismissed. A cannot thereafter claim possession of property as mortgagee as that ground ought to have been taken in the previous suit.

Similarly, wherein A files a suit against B to recover money on a pronote. B contends that the promissory note was obtained by undue influence. The objection is overruled and suit is decreed. B cannot challenge the promissory note on the ground of coercion or fraud in a subsequent suit, inasmuch as he ought to have taken that defence in the former suit.

4. IMPORTANT DEFINITIONS

4.1. Judgment, Decree and Order

The words Judgment, Decree and Order may be used interchangeably in common parlance, but in legal parlance each has a distinct meaning.

Judgment means the statement given by the Judge on the grounds of decree or order. It contains

(i) Concise statement of the case,

(ii) Points for determination,

(iii) Decision thereon, and

(iv) Reasons for such decision.

Decree means the formal expression of an adjudication which, so far as regards the Court expressing it, conclusively determines the rights of the parties with regard to all or any of the matters in controversy in the suit and may be either preliminary or final. It shall be deemed to include the rejection of a plaint and the determination of any question within section 144, but shall not include-

(a) any adjudication from which an appeal lies as an appeal from an order, or

(b) any order of dismissal for default.

To put simply, Decree follows Judgment. It is a formal document in a specified format and is prepared by the Official and signed by the Judge.

Order means formal expression of any decision of a Civil Court which is not a decree. For example, Order on application for Temporary Injunction, Appointment of Commissioner or Receiver, Dismissal of Suit in default, Restoration of Suit fall in domain of Order.

4.2. Legal Representative

The question of legal representative attains importance when party to a suit or proceeding dies and the question arise as to who shall come into his place for carrying on with the suit, appeal or execution of a decree. Simply put, the answer is legal representative.

Legal representative is a person who in law represents the estate of a deceased person. It includes

(i) any person who intermeddles with the estate of the deceased, and

(ii) where a party sues or is sued in a representative character the person on whom the estate devolves on the death of the party so suing or sued.

4.3. Mesne Profits

Mesne Profits of property means those profits which a person in wrongful possession of property actually received or might with ordinary diligence have received therefrom, together with interest on such profits. But it shall not include profits due to improvements made by the person in wrongful possession.

4.4. Caveat

Caveat means 'beware'. A person, apprehending that another person may institute a suit or file an application against him and obtain orders from Court, may file Caveat and claim right to appear before the Court on hearing of such suit or application.

The person filing the Caveat is called Caveator, and the person against whom it is filed is called Caveatee. Caveator shall serve a notice of Caveat by Registered Post acknowledgment due on the Caveatee.

Once a Caveat is duly filed, the court shall serve notice to the Caveator, as and when a suit or application is filed by the Caveatee. A caveat remains in force for a period of 90 days. If no application is filed within this period, the Caveat lapses.

4.5. Garnishee

Garnishee means Judgment Debtor's debtor. Garnishee becomes a person of interest where a judgment debtor in unwilling to discharge his obligation under money decree. In such cases, the Court may direct Garnishee to make good the payment upto the debt owned by him.

For example, a decree in favour of X and against Y is passed for payment of Rs. 10,000/-. G owes Y a sum of Rs. 5,000/-. X may apply to the Court for recovery of Rs. 5,000/- from G.

4.6. Precept

The authority of Civil Court is limited to the immovable properties situated in its territorial jurisdiction. Precept is a order of Court directing another Court to attach an immovable property situated in the jurisdiction of that other Court.

5. PRELIMINARY TOPICS

5.1. Pleadings, Plaint & Written Statement

CPC defines Pleadings as Plaint or written statement. Basically, Pleadings are statements in writing drawn up and filed by each party to a case, stating what his contentions will be at the trial, and giving all such details as his opponent to know, in order to prepare his case in answer. Plaint is filed by the Plaintiff, one who initiates suit. Written Statement is filed by the defendant, one who opposes plaintiff's claim.

Every pleading shall contain, and contain only a statement in a concise form of the material facts, on which the party pleading relies for his claim or defense, as the case may be, but not the evidence by which they are to be proved.

The purpose of pleading to set out clearly the assertions and claims of rival party with simplicity, brevity and precision, and without burdening it with the evidence or arguments or even the Law applicable.. The pleading is signed by the party and his advocate. Every pleading shall be verified at the foot by the party or by some other person proved to the satisfaction of the Court to be acquainted with the facts of the case.

A suit is instituted by filing of complaint. It is the foundation of the civil suit. A plaint contains the following -

(i) Heading : The name of the Court

(ii) Title : Name Description of Plaintiff and Defendant

(iii) Body : Material facts divided into paragraphs numbered consecutively.

(iv) Cause of Action

(v) Valuation and Court-fee paid

(vi) Court has Jurisdiction

(vii) Suit is within Limitation.

(viii) Relief sought

(ix) Signature and Verification

Written Statement is the defendant's answer to the plaint. The WS must contain parawise response to the plaint. The defendant must specifically deny the averments in the plaint, failing which he is deemed to have admitted the plaint's averments. The Defendant may further raise additional pleas including set-off and Counter claim.

Set-off is a plea whereby the defendant admits plaintiff's claim but states that certain sum is due towards him which must be adjusted against plaintiff's claim. Counter claim is essentially a counter suit, whereby the defendant not only denies plaintiff's claim but also seek counter relief. Thus the contents of a counter claim, thus, are same as a plaint.

5.2. Parties to the Suit

Plaintiff is the person who brings an action, while defendant defends it. An action is generally bought by one plaintiff against one defendant, but there may be situations where more than one person have similar rights. In such case, law permits joinder of parties.

In case of plaintiffs, all persons may be joined as plaintiffs in one suit, if the relief claimed arises from same act or transaction and if separate suits were brought any common question of law or fact would arise. Similarly, all persons may be joined as defendants when any relief claimed arises out of same act or transaction, and if separate suits were brought any common question of law or fact would arise.

For example, A company A ltd. brought an Initial Public Offer (IPO). X,Y and Z believed the statements in the prospectus and bought shares of the Company. The statements were in fact a misrepresentation. X,Y and Z may jointly sue Company A.

Similarly, where a passenger A is injured in a collision between B's bus and C's truck, A may sue B and C jointly for damages since there is one transaction and the suit involves common question of law and fact.

5.3. Issue & Service of Summons

Summon means an order of appearance. Summons is a formal court document embodying the order. When a plaint is registered as suit, the Court issues summons to the defendant as an information of institution of suit and with a view to solicit his response. Summons are

The summons are generally issued through Court's designated agency of process servers. To expedite the process, summons may also be issued through registered post acknowledgment due, speed post, High Court approved Courier Service, fax or email.

The summons are served on the party in person, and in his absence upon an adult family member (but not a servant) residing in the same household. Where the defendant refuses to sign the acknowledgment, or where the serving officer, after using all due and reasonable diligence, cannot find the defendant, who is absent from his residence at the time when service is sought to be effected on him at his residence and there is no likelihood of his being found at the residence within a reasonable time and there is no agent or any other person on whom service can be made the serving officer shall affix a copy of the summons on the outer door or some other conspicuous part of the house in which the defendant ordinarily resides or carries on business or personally works for gain.

Where there is reason to believe that the defendant is avoiding service of summons, the Court may orders service by an advertisement in a daily newspaper circulating in the locality.

5.4. Non appearance of Parties

There may arise situations where one or more party does not appear before the Court on any date fixed. In such cases, CPC provides specific rules as to the effect of non-appearance. They are summarized as below.

On non-appearance of both plaintiff and defendant, or where only the defendant appears, the suit is dismissed for default. In such cases, the plaintiff may apply for restoration by showing sufficient cause for non-appearance.

Where plaintiff appears but the defendant does not appear despite service of summons, the suit is proceeded ex-parte. The Court records the evidence for the plaintiff and pronounce its judgment. The decree herein is called ex-parte. The defendant, too, may apply for setting aside ex-parte decree by showing sufficient cause for non-appearance.

6.SOME IMPORTANT CONCEPTS

6.1. Temporary Injunction

Injunction is a court order refraining a party from doing or directing a party to do some particular act. Injunction may be temporary or perpetual in duration. Perpetual injunction is granted by decree of Civil Court made at the hearing and on the merits of the case. Perpetual Injunction is governed by the Specific Relief Act. Temporary injunctions are those that continue for a specified time or until further orders of the courts. CPC enables courts to grant temporary injunctions.

A Temporary Injunction may be granted in following circumstances -

(a) The property in dispute is in danger of being wasted, damaged or alienated by any party to the suit, or wrongfully sold in execution of a decree.

(b) The defendant threatens, or intends, to remove or dispose of his property with a view to defraud his creditors.

(c) The defendant threatens to dispossess the plaintiff or otherwise cause injury to the plaintiff in relation to the property in dispute.

The Court may by order grant a temporary injunction to restrain such act, or make such other order for the purpose of staying and preventing the wasting, damaging, alienation, sale, removal or disposition of the property or dispossession of the plaintiff, or otherwise causing injury to the plaintiff in relation to any property in dispute in the suit as the Court thinks fit until the disposal of the suit or until further orders.

Illustrations

(i) A is attempting to demolish his neighbour B's wall and encroach upon his land. B may sue for perpetual injunction and also apply for temporary injunction.

(ii) Trustee T is attempting to sell trust property in violation of the trust deed. Beneficiary B may sue for enforcement of Trust and inter alia apply for temporary injunction.

6.2. Commissions

Certain acts cannot be performed within the four walls of the Court Room and the Court may have to ascertain facts which cannot be brought to it. Thus, the Court is empowered to issue Commission for following purposes -

(a) to examine any person;

(b) to make a local investigation;

(c) to examine or adjust accounts;

(d) to make a partition;

(e) to hold a scientific, technical, or expert investigation;

(f) to conduct sale of property which is subject to speedy and natural decay and which is in the custody of the Court pending the determination of the suit;

(g) to perform any ministerial act.

The Court while issuing commission, appoints a Commissioner, who is generally Court Amin or an Advocate but in special circumstances any other expert may also be appointed. The Court gives specific instructions for execution of commission and Commissioner files its compliance report in the Court.

6.3. Receiver

There may arise situations where the property in is dispute must be looked after by some person, other than the parties. In such cases, the Court has power to appoint a Receiver. He may be empowered to take over possession and management, protect, preserve or make improvement, collect and apply rents or profits, and execute documents ordered by the Court.

The purpose of appointment of receiver is to save the property from being wasted owing to the rival claims of the parties. For example, where there are rival claims as to management of trust property, the Court may appoint a receiver, as in such cases the parties may have tendency to elucidate personal gains out of the same.

6.4. Death of a Party, Substitution and Abatement

CPC has provisions for creation, transfer and devolution of interests in pending cases. The two cardinal rules are -

First, a personal cause of action dies with the person,

Second, if the right to sue survives, the death of a party (plaintiff or defendant) does not cause the suit to abate.

For example, A sues his wife B for divorce. During pendency of suit, A or B dies. The suit abates, since divorce is a personal cause of action. The legal heirs cannot step into the shoes of the parties to the suit.

But where a person A sues B for compensation due to injury caused. Death of either party will not abate the suit. The legal heirs of A or B (as the case may be) shall be substituted in place of original parties to proceed with the litigation. However, B's legal representative shall be liable only to the extent of the property of the deceased inherited by him.

It is pertinent to note that since the suit proceeds on the initiation of the plaintiff, it is the duty of the plaintiff to move substitution application on the death of the defendant, and it is the duty of the legal representatives of the plaintiff to approach the Court on the death of the plaintiff. The time frame within which substitution application must be moved is 90 days from the death of party, failingly the suit stands abated in respect of the deceased.

6.5. Alternate Dispute Resolution

Often it has been observed that even after pronouncement of judgment by the Court, the dispute stands. The reason is that the Court merely pronounce Judgment of facts before itself but does not resolve the dispute, which often involve factors beyond judicial determination. Thus, Civil procedure provides for Alternate Dispute Resolution (or ADR) Mechanism.

The Civil Court may, in appropriate cases, refer the dispute for Arbitration, Conciliation, Judicial settlement including settlement through Lok Adalat, or Mediation.

Arbitration is adjudicatory hearing by a private Arbitrator or a panel of Arbitrators. It is similar to Court adjudication, but it can be made only where exists a written agreement to that effect. It is suitable in cases pertaining to commerce, where dispute involves Expert Adjudication.

Conciliation is aimed at reconciling of the dispute by Expert Conciliator. Conciliation is an intermix of arbitration and mediation. The chief difference with arbitration is that a party to Conciliation may withdraw its consent at any stage of the proceedings, and the conciliation proceedings come to a halt at that very moment.

Judicial Settlement and Lok Adalat are Court assisted methods to arrive at a compromise between the parties.

Mediation involves active assistance to the parties to arrive at a workable solution to the dispute. This is a preferred mode of ADR in family matters.

6.6. Withdrawal

A Civil litigation litigation proceeds at the instance of the Plaintiff. Thus, the Plaintiff may withdraw his suit or abandon part of his claim as against all or any of the defendants. If the plaintiff withdraws without the permission of court, he is liable for costs and is precluded from instituting any fresh suit.

But, when the Court is satisfied that a suit must fail by reason of some formal defect, or, that there are other sufficient grounds for allowing the plaintiff to institute a fresh suit for the subject matter of a suit then it may grant permission to withdraw the suit with the liberty to institute a fresh suit.

6.7. Compromise

A Civil litigation is a lis between the parties with little impact on public interests. Thus, the parties to a litigation are allowed to enter into a compromise as respect the matter in dispute.

Where the Court is satisfied that the suit has been adjusted fully or partly by a lawful agreement or compromise in writing and signed by the parties to the suit, or the defendant satisfies the plaintiff in respect of the whole or any part of the subject-matter of the suit, the court shall record such agreement, compromise or satisfaction, and shall pass a decree in accordance therewith.

No consent decree is passed if the agreement or compromise made by the parties is void or voidable under the Contract Act. The consent decree is not appealable. Also, no suit shall lie to set aside a decree on the ground that the compromise on which the decree is based was not lawful.

In representative suits, compromise cannot be entered into without the leave of the Court. Before granting such leave, the Court shall give notice to persons interested in the suit.

7. SPECIAL SUITS

7.1. Suits against Government

Generally, the law does not mandate giving of notice to the defendant before institution of suit. However, the Government, whether of the Union or the State, the Railways and Public Officer, enjoy a privilege that before institution of suit, a two months notice must be served upon them. The object is to provide an opportunity to the Government to reconsider the legal position, and to amend or settle the claim without any litigation.

In suits against Central Government, Railways, State Government or Public Officer, the said notice shall be given to Secretary, General Manager, Secretary / District Collector or the Public Officer respectively.

The notice shall be in writing. It shall state the name, description, place of residence of the plaintiff, cause of action and the relief claimed.

It is pertinent to note that a suit to obtain an urgent or immediate relief against the Government or any public officer may be instituted, with the leave of the Court, without serving the aforesaid notice or within the period of two months after the notice is given. In such cases, the Court decides whether the case involves urgency. If the Court finds otherwise, the plaint is returned for presentation after compliance of the said two months notice.

7.2. Suits by indigent person or Pauper Suit

Law mandates payment of Court fee at certain rate having regard to the value of property in dispute and relief claimed. The said fee is payable by the plaintiff on the institution of suit. But there may arise situations where the party is not in position to do so. At the same time, he cannot be denied his right to seek redressal of grievance before the Civil Court.

A person who is not possessed of sufficient means (other than the property in dispute) to pay the prescribed court fee for the suit is called Indigent.

Every application for leave (permission) to sue as indigent must contain the particulars of a plaint and also a schedule of any movable or immovable property belonging to the applicant with its estimated value. The Court issues notice to the opposite party and Government pleader. Court may also record evidence to ascertain whether the applicant is indigent or not.

If the applicant is allowed, the payment of Court fee is not exempted but is merely deferred till disposal of the suit. Where the plaintiff succeeds in the suit, the Court shall calculate the amount of Court-fees and such amount shall be recoverable by the State Government from any party ordered by the decree to pay the same, Where the plaintiff fails in the suit the Court shall order the plaintiff to pay the court-fees.

7.3. Suit by or Against Minor, Next friend and Guardian ad litem

A minor is presumed incapable of effectively preserving his rights before the Courts and thus the law provides for a protection mechanism in form of Next Friend and Guardian ad litem. Next friend is a person acting for Minor plaintiff and Guardian ad litem is a person acting for Minor defendant.

Next friend or Guardian are not parties to the suit unless they are parties in their own capacity, that is co-plaintiff or co-defendant. Any person of the age of majority and of sound mind may be appointed as Next friend or Guardian, provided they have no adverse interest with the minor they act for.

7.4. Representative Suits

Representative suit is an exception to the general rule that all persons interested in a suit ought to be impleaded. When a large number of persons have a community of interest, some of them may approach the Court for themselves as well as on behalf of others. Such a suit is called representative suit.

The Court may permit as well as direct that one or more of the numerous persons having same interest in a suit sue or be sued for benefit of all. In such cases, the Court gives notice to all the concerned persons either personally or by public advertisement. Such interested person may apply to the Court to be made a party.

A decree in a representative suit shall be binding on all persons represented and acts as res judicata for future litigation. Also, no part of the suit shall be withdrawn or abandoned or compromised without notice to all concerned.

8. REVIEW AND REVISION

8.1. Review

Review means to re-consider. CPC provides for review of a decision by the very court which passed the decree or made the order. Any person considering himself aggrieved by a decree or order may apply for a review of judgment to the Court which passed the decree or made the order, and the Court may make such order thereon as it thinks fit.

It is important that review is permissible only when appeal is not allowed, or if allowed, is not preferred. There cannot be simultaneous review and appeal from order or decree.

8.2. Revision

Law provides that each Court must exercise its jurisdiction strictly according to the law. To achieve this end, law provides for a hierarchical structure, wherein a Superior Court is authorized to revise orders of Subordinate Court where the Subordinate Court has -

(i) exercised a jurisdictin not vested in it by law,

(ii) failed to exercise a jurisdiction so vested, or

(iii) acted in exercise of its jurisdiction illegally or with material irregularity.

Again, the order must be non-appealable. Revisional Jurisdiction cannot be exercised where appeal may be preferred by the aggrieved party.

9. APPEALS

Appeal literally means request. It is a request by an aggrieved party to examine the validity or propriety of an order or judgment. Appeal is a substantive right and not procedural. It is a statutory right and is permissible only in cases provided by the statute.

9.1. Appeal from Original Decree

Appeal from Original Decree is also termed as First appeal. An appeal lies from every decree passed by any Court exercising original jurisdiction to the Court authorized to hear appeals. Appeal may be filed against an original decree passed ex parte. But no appeal lies from a consent-decree.

Also, no appeal lies from a small causes court if value of the subject matter is upto Rs. 10,000/- except on a question of law.

Further, in cases where a preliminary decree has been passed and the same is not challenged in appeal, the aggrieved party cannot challenge its correctness in any appeal from final decree.

9.2. Second Appeals

Code of Civil Procedure provides for appeal to the High Court from every decree passed by the appellate court, if the High Court is satisfied that the case involves a substantial question of law. The memorandum of appeal should precisely state the substantial question of law involved. If satisfied, the Court formulates that question of law and the appeal is heard by the High Court on that question. The respondent is allowed to argue that the case involves no substantial question of law.

9.3. Appeal from Orders

Unlike Judgments or decrees, which are appealable as a rule, not all orders are appealable. CPC provides a list of orders against which an appeal may be filed. Further, interlocutory orders are non-appealable as a general rule. Interlocutory orders are those that do not affect the rights of the parties nor rule on them but are passed on day to day basis for furtherance of the proceedings.

10. INHERENT POWERS OF COURT

Procedural Law, howsoever elaborate, cannot be exhaustive in all aspects. Thus, the Courts are accorded Inherent powers to make such orders as may be necessary for the ends of justice, or to prevent abuse of the process of the Court. This inherent power has not been conferred on the Court by Code of Civil Procedure. It is a power inherent in the Court itself, by virtue of its duty to do justice between the parties before it.

When there are no express provisions in CPC and where the circumstances demand, the Court may act upon the assumption of its inherent power in the interests of justice. Some examples of Inherent Powers are as follows -

(i) Joint trail of suits,

(ii) Apply principles of res judicata otherwise than section 11 of the act,

(iii) Rectification of mistakes,

(iv) Amend sale certification or correct description of property.

(v) Punish disobedience of Court order, etc.

But inherent powers cannot be exercised to do what is prohibited by CPC. The Court can neither extend period of limitation nor entertain a suit which is not of Civil nature. Also, the inherent power should not be exercised in derogation of express provisions of CPC.

CRIMINAL PROCEDURE

1. Introduction

The object of the Criminal Procedural Law is to provide a mechanism for prevention and detection of, and punishment for criminal acts. In India, Code of Criminal Procedure, 1973 (or CrPC) is the chief enactment that lays down the rules for conduct of investigation into offences by the police and proceedings in court against any person who has committed an offence under IPC or under any other law. The same has

1.1. CLASSIFICATION OF OFFENCES

CrPC classifies offences in IPC under various categories for the sake of simplicity. The classification is as follows -

1.1.1. Bailable and Non-bailable offences:

Offences are classified as bailable and non-bailable, depending upon the right of accused to obtain bail. Schedule I to CrPC enumerates whether the offence is bailable or not. As a general rule, an offence punishable with maximum imprisonment of 3 years or more is non-bailable, while those punishable with lesser sentence are bailable. Thus, severity of sentence is the basis of this classification. Minor offences are bailable. In such cases, an accused has a right to obtain bail during the pendency of investigation or trial.

On the other hand non-bailable offences are serious and grave offences (say for example Murder, Rape, Robbery, Forgery, etc) where the accused does not have a right to obtain bail. In such cases, bail is granted only on the discretion of the Court.

1.1.2. Cognizable and non-cognizable offences:

Cognizable offences are those in which police officer can investigate and arrest an accused person without obtaining a warrant from the Court. Theses are serious offences requiring immediate action. For example, Murder, Rape, Theft, etc.

In non-cognizable offences, the police must obtain orders from the Magistrate before proceeding with the investigation or making an arrest. Say for example Defamation.

1.1.3. Compoundable and non-compoundable offences:

Yet another classification of offence is based on whether the offence can be compounded or not. Compound means mutual settlement.

As a general rule, a crime is an act against the society. But certain offences affect only a few individuals rather than the society as a whole. Their impact is very limited.

For such offences, it is provided that the victim and the assailant may come to terms, and conclude the trial. Offences may be compoundable, compoundable with the permission of the Court, or non-compoundable altogether. The list is enumerated in S. 320 of CrPC.

2. STAGES OF CRIMINAL PROCEDURE

Criminal Procedure comes into action even before commission of an offence. The law provides that it the duty of the Police to take preventive action against commission of offence and maintain law and order. But it is not always possible to prevent the same. Hence, a machinery is required to prosecute, punish and bring the perpetrator to Justice. As per CrPC, it involves three major stages – Investigation, Inquiry, and Trial.

Firstly, the police investigates into a complaint / information (or FIR) made by a victim or any other person, and files a Report. Secondly, based on the report of the police, the magistrate inquires whether there is sufficient ground to proceed with the prosecution. Thirdly, the state prosecutes the accused at a criminal trial where the accused may either be convicted (found guilty), or acquitted (found not-guilty).

These three stages are discussed in following pages.

3. INVESTIGATION

Investigation is a preliminary stage conducted by the police (or other specialized detective agencies such as CBI). Investigation begins with the registration of First Information Report (FIR) at the police station. Anyone - not only the victim - can notify the police about the commission of an offence by recording an FIR.

If, from the FIR, the officer-in-charge of a police station suspects that an offence has been committed he is duty-bound to investigate the same. Investigation primarily consists of ascertaining facts and circumstances of the case. Investigation includes the following -

(a) Proceeding to the spot

(b) Ascertainment facts and circumstances

(c) Collection of evidence – Documentary or Material

(d) Recording of statement of witnesses and accused

(e) Discovery and arrest of the suspected offender

(f) Search of places

(g) Seizure of things including weapon of offence

(h) Formation of opinion as to whether the case is made out.

(i) If yes, filing of the charge-sheet. If no case is made out, or the accused cannot be ascertained, filing of closure / summary / final report.

Investigation ends in a police report to the magistrate.

As a matter of common experience, the police often refuses to register an FIR. It must be noted that the Station Officer is duty bound to register an FIR on the information of cognizable offence. If he refuses to or abstains from or procrastinate, one may make an application before Superintendent of Police. Further, an application u/s 156(3) CrPC may be moved before the Magistrate having jurisdiction to take cognizance in the matter.

Another course of action is that the person can proceed directly to file a complaint before the Magistrate.

4. INQUIRY

Inquiry refers to every proceeding done by a Magistrate which is not a trial. It is a judicial proceeding conducted by the Magistrate or Court to determine whether the further proceedings are required and should the case move to trial.

Ordinarily, it is midway stage between Police Investigation and Trial. The magistrate examines the Police Investigation Report (Charge Sheet / Final Report) and decides whether there is sufficient ground to proceed to trial. It is worth noting that the Magistrate is not bound by the conclusion of the Investigating Officer. The Magistrate may accept the report as it is, or send for further investigation in case of charge sheet. In case of final report, the Magistrate accept it, and the case comes to an end. If he finds lapses in investigation, order further investigation. Or if he finds sufficient material may take cognizance directly. As an alternative, he may take cognizance as complaint and record the evidence of the witnesses, and pass summoning order on the basis of the same.

A magistrate also makes an inquiry in complaints filed directly before him. A person, may instead of approaching the Police, move a complaint before the magistrate for his taking action. Also, in non-cognizable offences, a person needs to approach the magistrate for appropriate action.

In short, the object of inquiry is to judge whether there is ground to proceed for trial.

5. TRIAL

Trial is the judicial adjudication of a person's guilt or innocence. There are following four kinds of trials in CrPC – Session Trial, Warrant Trial, Summon Trial and Summary Trials.

As a norm, offences punishable with death, life imprisonment or imprisonment for a term exceeding seven years are triable exclusively by Sessions Court. The trial of such cases is conducted in a Sessions Court after the case is committed or forwarded to it by a Magistrate.

A warrant case relates to an offences punishable with death or imprisonment for a term greater than two years. The CrPC provides for two types of procedure for the trial of warrant cases by a magistrate viz. Cases instituted upon a police report, and cases instituted upon complaint.

In respect of cases instituted on police report, the magistrate may "discharge" the accused upon consideration of the police report and documents sent with it. The Magistrate need not hear the prosecution or record further evidence.

In respect of the cases instituted otherwise than on police report, the magistrate is bound to hear the prosecution and record evidence. If no case is made out, the accused is discharged.

In both cases, if the accused is not discharged, the magistrate holds a regular trial after "framing the charge".

A summons case relates to offences punishable with imprisonment of upto two years. Framing of a formal charge is not mandatory in summons case. However, the court must give the substance of the accusation, called "notice", to the accused. Since framing of charge is not mandatory, there is no hearing on charge, nor the accused be discharged in the case. A summons case may be converted into a warrant case in the interest of justice.

In order to save time and expense, CrPC also provides for summary trial of petty offences. The trial is conducted in summary manner. That is the recording of evidence is not verbatim and the judgment is also in brief.

Apart from these, CrPC also provides that in cases punishable with fine only, the court may issue special summons wherein the party may plead guilty by payment of fine even without entering appearance in the court. In case, he wishes to contest, he may appear before the court and plead the same.

6. STAGES IN CRIMINAL TRIAL

Although each trial mentioned herein-before has its peculiar features, there are certain common elements in each criminal trial. These common features or stages are

(a) Framing of Charge

(b) Prosecution Evidence

(c) Statement of accused

(d) Defence Evidence

(e) Final Arguments

(f) Judgment

(g) Sentence, in case of conviction

6.1. Framing of charge and Pleading thereto

Charge framing is the beginning of a trial. Charge means formal accusation of the offence. The Court examines the Case Diary (from the Investigation Report of the Police) and ascertains whether or not a prima facie case against the accused has been made out.

Charged is framed on basis of the material available before the Court from Investigation and Inquiry.

If, on the contrary, the Court considers the materials insufficient for proceeding against the accused, the Court shall discharge the accused and record its reasons for doing so.

The charge is read over and explained to the accused who may plead guilty or not-guilty. If the accused pleads guilty, the judge shall record the plea and may convict him. If the accused pleads not guilty and claims trial, the trial begins.

Charge is the beginning of the trial. All proceeding before framing of charge before the Court is called inquiry.

Charge is the basis of criminal trial. It sets out the offence that was allegedly committed, and for which the accused stands a chance for conviction and punishment. An accused may be convicted for a lesser offence, but he can never be convicted for an offence greater than the one charged. Although, the Court may alter charge at any stage and in such cases the accused has a right to cross-examine witnesses already examined.

6.2. Prosecution evidence

After the charge is framed, the prosecution is asked to examine its witnesses before the court. Witnesses are examined on oath. Recording of oral evidence of witness has three stages – Examination-in-Chief, Cross Examination and Re-examination.

Examination-in-chief is conducted by the party calling the witness. That is, the party who has produced the witness is questioned by that party or his counsel itself. The purpose of examination-in-chief is to elicit all the material facts from the witness within his knowledge which tend to prove the party's case.

Cross-examination is an examination of a witness which is done by the adverse party (herein accused) after the examination-in-chief. The purpose of the cross-examination is to ascertain the truthfulness of the witness and to raise doubt or suspicion over his testimony. On rare occasions, a counsel may also elucidate a statement favouring the accused.

Re-examination is an examination of a witness by the party calling the witness after the cross-examination. Its purpose is to remove incompatibility or inconsistency which arises during the examination-in-chief and cross-examination. The accused may further cross-examine a witness after re-examination, if any.

As a norm, recording of evidence should be continued day-to-day until all the witnesses in attendance have been examined.

6.3. Statement of accused

The court may examine the accused at any stage of inquiry or trial for the purpose of eliciting any explanation against incriminating circumstances appearing before it. However, it is mandatory for the court to question the accused after completion of prosecution evidence.

This examination is without oath and before the accused enters a defence. The purpose of this examination is to give the accused a reasonable opportunity to explain incriminating facts and circumstances in the case.

6.4. Defence evidence

If after taking the evidence for the prosecution, examining the accused and hearing the prosecution and defence, the judge considers that there is no evidence that the accused has committed the offence, the judge is required to record the order of acquittal. However, when the accused is not acquitted for absence of evidence, a defence must be entered and evidence adduced in its support. For this purpose, the defence may examine witnesses including the accused. The witnesses produced by the defence are cross-examined by the prosecution.

Most accused persons do not lead defence evidence in India. One of the major reasons for this is that in India, the burden is cast on the prosecution to prove the offence and the degree of proof required in a criminal trial is "proof beyond reasonable doubt". This is quite a high standard that the prosecution must meet. It is not enough for the prosecution to assert that the accused has committed the offence. The judge must be convinced beyond reasonable doubt that it was in fact the accused who committed the offence.

6.5. Final arguments

This is the final stage of the trial. The provisions of the CrPC provide that when examination of the witnesses for the defence (if any) is complete, the prosecutor shall sum up the prosecution case and the accused is entitled to reply. These are the final arguments.

6.6. Judgment

After the final arguments by the prosecutor and defence, the judge pronounces his judgment in the trial. Under the CrPC, an accused can be withdrawn from prosecution at any stage of trial with the permission of the court. If the accused is allowed to be withdrawn from prosecution prior to framing of charge, this is a discharge, while in cases where such withdrawal is allowed after framing of charge, it is acquittal.

LAW OF EVIDENCE

1. Introduction

In common parlance, Evidence refers to an outward sign or an indication. Law of Evidence, contained in the Indian Evidence Act, stipulates how facts can be proved through evidence. The Evidence Act helps the judges to separate the 'wheat from the chaff' and plays a crucial role in the establishment of facts during the court proceedings.

Before going further, one needs to understand the use of term "Fact". Fact means any thing, state of things, relation of things, or any mental condition. Thus, legally a fact may be physical as well as psychological.

"Fact in Issue" means any fact from which the existence, non-existence, nature or extent of any right, liability, or disability, asserted or denied in any suit or proceeding, necessarily follows. For example, in a murder trial the fact in issue is the fact of murder by the accused. Similarly, in a civil suit, fact in issue refer to claims of each party.

One fact is evidence of another when it tends in any degree to render the existence of that other probable. The quality by virtue of which it has such an effect may be called its probative force, and evidence may therefore be defined as any fact which possesses such force. Probative force may be of any degree of intensity. When it is great enough to form a rational basis for the inference that the fact so evidenced really exists, the evidence possessing it is said to constitute proof.

Now, we shall discuss, following important aspects of law of evidence -

(a) Relevancy

(b) Admissibility of Evidence

(c) Rule against Hearsay

(d) Rule of Best Evidence

(e) Presumption

(f) Burden of Proof

(g) Competency of Witness

(h) Privileged Communication

(i) Examination of Witness

(j) Leading Questions

1.1. Relevancy of Evidence

Evidence must not be far-fetched. It must be relevant to the fact in issue. A fact is relevant when it has reasonable connection to the fact in issue. Reasonable in the sense that in common prudence existence of one fact renders the other fact probable. Per Bentham, one fact is relevant to another, if the effect or tendency of the former when presented to the mind, is to produce a persuasion concerning the existence of some other matter of fact. Rules of relevancy are based on logic, and only a relevant evidence may be taken on record.

Based on logic, the law provides that things done in same transaction (res gestae), cause, effect, occasion, conduct of parties, alibi, admission, confession, facts showing the existence of any state of mind, similar occurrences, natural course of business, dying declarations, are regarded as relevant.

Surprisingly, as a general rule, Judgments and orders of Court are not relevant evidence. Where a Judgment creates a bar on new proceedings, or where any legal character is conferred by Probate, Matrimonial Admiralty or Insolvency Court, they are relevant evidence.

Similarly, opinions of persons are not regarded as evidence, since different person may hold different opinion of things and situation. But opinion of an expert in context of a foreign law, science, art, handwriting, or finger impressions is regarded as relevant.

1.2. Admissibility

Admissibility refers to the process whereby the court determines whether the law of evidence permits that relevant evidence, to be received by the court or not. Rules of admissibility are strict legal principles within which the Court decides whether or not the evidence adduced be relied upon.

It is pertinent to note that relevancy is a precondition of admissibility. Rule against Hearsay and Rule of Best Evidence are the chief doctrines of admissibility.

1.3. Rule against Hearsay

Hearsay means heard what others say. The term *hearsay* denotes a kind of evidence which does not derive its value solely from the credit given to the witness himself, but which rests also, in part, on the veracity and competence of some other person.

Law of Evidence states that the Oral evidence must be direct in all cases whatever. That is, if it refers to a fact which could be seen, it must be the evidence of a witness who says he saw it. If it refers to a fact which could be heard, it must be the evidence of a witness who says he heard it. If it refers to a fact which could be perceived by any other sense or in any other manner, it must be the evidence of a witness who says he perceived it by that sense or in that manner. Thus, hearsay is inadmissible.

The rationale behind the provision is that the account given by a person other than the one who witnessed the event is an adulterated and unreliable one. Evidence of a statement made to a witness by a person who is not himself called as witness may or may not be hearsay. It is hearsay and *inadmissible* when the object of the evidence is to establish the truth of what is contained in the statement.

Some important exception to the rule are res gestae, admission, confession, dying declaration, and evidence given in formal proceedings.

1.4. Rule of Best Evidence

Rule of Best Evidence pertains to documentary evidence. Documentary Evidence is of two kinds – Primary and Secondary. Primary means the Document itself. Secondary evidence means and includes -

(1) certified copies given under the provisions hereinafter contained;

(2) copies made from the original by mechanical processes which in themselves insure the accuracy of the copy, and copies compared with such copies;

(3) copies made from or compared with the original;

(4) counterparts of documents as against the parties who did not execute them;

(5) oral accounts of the contents of a document given by some person who has himself seen it.

Rule of Best Evidence states that when the terms of a contract, grant, or any other disposition of property, have been reduced to the form of a document, and where any matter is required by law to be reduced to the form of a document, no evidence shall be given in proof of the terms of such contract, grant or other disposition of property, except the document itself, or secondary evidence of its contents in cases in which secondary evidence is admissible.

The basis of this rule is that when parties have deliberately put their agreement into writing, it is conclusively presumed that they intended the writing to form final statement of their intentions and that it should be placed beyond the reach of future controversy, faith and treacherous memory.

Further, the rule excludes admission of oral evidence of variance. Once a document has been produced no evidence of any oral agreement or statement, for the purpose of contradicting, varying, adding to or subtracting from its terms shall be admissible.

There are following exceptions to this rule -

(a) When a public officer is required by law to be appointed in writing, and any officer has acted as such, the writing need not be proved

(b) Will admitted to probate may be proved by the probate

(c) Facts which invalidates the document

(d) Matters on which document is silent

(e) Condition precedent

(f) Subsequent rescission or modification

(g) Usage or customs not mentioned in but annexed to contract

(h) Manner in which the language in a document has been used.

1.5. Presumption

Presumption means taken for granted. In evidence, Presumptions are inferences drawn on the validity or truth of a thing. Presumption operates as proof of a fact even when there is no any complete evidence of its existence.

Law provides for presumption in three form – May, Shall and Conclusive Proof.

Whenever it is provided that the Court may presume a fact, it may either regard such fact as proved, unless and until it is disproved, or may call for proof of it.

Whenever it is directed that the Court shall presume a fact, it shall regard such fact as proved, unless and until it is disproved.

When one fact is declared to be conclusive proof of another, the Court shall, on proof of the one fact, regard the other as proved, and shall not allow evidence to be given for the purpose of disproving it.

The "May" and "Shall" presumptions are regarded as rebuttable as the affected party is allowed to adduce evidence to the contrary, thereby defeating the presumption. While "Conclusive Proof" is an irrebuttable presumption as it debars the party to adduce a contrary evidence.

Some common presumptions under Indian Evidence Act are as follows -

(a) Court shall presume certified copy to be genuine;

(b) Court shall presume maps, plans or charts made by the Central Government to be accurate;

(c) Court shall presume that secure electronic record has not been altered;

(d) Court may presume valid execution of 20 year old document produced from proper custody;

(e) When a person has not been heard of dead or alive for seven or more years shall be presumed to be dead;

(f) Person in possession of property is presumed to be the owner;

(g) Birth of a child during continuance of valid marriage or within 280 days of its dissolution is conclusive proof of legitimacy;

(h) Court may presume that a man in possession of stolen goods soon after the theft is either the thief or has received the goods knowing them to be stolen, unless he can account for his possession;

(i) Court may presume that judicial and official acts have been regularly performed;

(j) Court may presume that evidence which could be and is not produced would, if produced, be unfavourable to the person who withholds it;

(k) Court may presume that if a man refuses to answer a question, the answer, if given, would be unfavourable to him;

(l) Court may presume that when a document creating an obligation is in the hands of the obligor, the obligation has been discharged.

1.6. Burden of Proof

Burden of Proof is an expression used for who shall prove a fact before the Court. It refers to the legal requirement or responsibility of the parties to establish the facts that will assist the court in reaching a decision in their favour.

The general rule as to Burden of Proof is - Whoever desires any Court to give judgment as to any legal right or liability dependent on the existence of facts which he asserts, must prove that those facts exist. When a person is bound to prove the existence of any fact, it is said that the burden of proof lies on that person.

There is a similar and inter-woven concept of burden to adduce evidence. While burden of proof is constant, burden to adduce evidence is of shifting nature. Burden to adduce evidence lies on the party who would fail if no evidence at all were given on either side.

It is pertinent to note here that when a presumption exists in favour of a party, the burden to prove the contrary is on the opposite party.

1.7. Competency of Witness

Law of Evidence provides that the witness must be competent. That is to say, he must be capable of understanding the questions put to him and give rational answers to them.

All persons are competent to testify unless the Court considers that they are prevented from understanding the questions put to them, or from giving rational answers to those questions, by tender, years, extreme old age, disease, whether of body or mind, or any other cause of the same kind.

Even a lunatic is not incompetent to testify, unless he is prevented by his lunacy from understanding the questions put to him and giving rational answers to them. A dumb witness may give evidence by writing or by use of signs.

An accomplice is also a competent witness against an accused but his evidence is regarded as unworthy of credit unless he is corroborated in material particulars.

1.8. Privileged Communication

Certain communications are regarded as privileged under the law of evidence. The basis of the rule is that certain relationships are so private that even the law should recognise the confidentiality of their interactions.

Some of the privileged communications are -

(a) Communication between Husband and Wife during subsistence of marriage

(b) Professional Communication between Legal Practitioner and Client

(c) Communication to Public officer made to him in official confidence

(d) Police Officer and Identity of Informer of commission of offence

1.9. Examination of Witness

Examination of Witness involves three stages, namely – Examination-in-Chief, Cross Examination and Re-examination.

The examination of a witness by the party who calls him is called his examination-in-chief.

The examination of a witness by the adverse party is called his cross-examination.

The further examination of a witness by the party who called him, subsequent to the cross-examination, is called re-examination.

The order of examinations is that a witness is first examined-in-chief. Then cross-examined on the desire of adverse party. Further, if the party so desires re-examination is done.

The purpose of re-examination is to solicit explanation of matters referred to in cross examination. If any new matter is introduced in re-examination, the adverse party may further cross-examine the witness.

Code of Civil Procedure permits examination-in-chief to be filed by way of affidavit.

1.10 Leading Questions

Leading questions pertain to the domain of examination of witness. It is common practice for advocates to put forth questions to a witness in such a manner to obtain desirable answers. To this end, leading questions are employed.

A leading question is one suggesting the answer which the person putting it wishes or expects to receive.

If the adverse party objects, leading questions cannot be asked in examination-in-chief or in a re-examination. Because the account of the incident must come from the mouth of the witness and not the advocate.

Since the purpose of cross-examination is to test the veracity of statement of the witness, leading questions may be asked in there-in.

At times, a witness may turn hostile. That either he denies knowledge or gives evidence contradictory to the interest of the party who has called the witness. In such situations, even the party calling the witness is allowed to put leading questions that practically amounts to cross-examination by the party calling the witness.

*** *** ***